A GARDENER'S GUIDE TO
TOPIARY

A GARDENER'S GUIDE TO
TOPIARY

the art of clipping, training and shaping plants

JENNY HENDY
photographed by Steven Wooster

LORENZ BOOKS

This edition is published by Lorenz Books
an imprint of Anness Publishing Ltd
info@anness.com
www.lorenzbooks.com
www.annesspublishing.com

© Anness Publishing Ltd 2021

A CIP catalogue record for this book is available from the British Library.

Publisher: Joanna Lorenz
Editorial Director: Judith Simons
Executive Editor: Caroline Davison
Project Editor: Katy Bevan
Designer: Lisa Tai
Photographer: Steven Wooster
Production Controller: Ben Worley

Publisher's note

The authors and the publisher have made every effort to ensure that all

instructions contained in this book are accurate and that the safest methods

are recommended. Readers should follow all recommended safety procedures

and wear protective goggles and gloves and clothing at all times during the

cutting and trimming of hedges, for example. You should know how to use all

your tools and equipment safely and make sure you are confident about what

you are doing. The publisher and author cannot accept liability for any resulting

injury, damage or loss to persons or property as a result of using any

equipment in this book or carrying out any of the projects.

CONTENTS

Left Topiary is an outlet for artistic expression and the many different forms not only add structure but also a great deal of character to gardens.

Right Simple geometric shapes are easy to produce and, clipped from plants like box that give a fine-textured finish, they look striking against untamed foliage and flowers.

INTRODUCTION

Many people still imagine topiary to be something practised exclusively by skilled gardeners in the employ of the landed gentry. However, it has always had a folk art following among country people and is rapidly becoming a pastime that is fun and accessible for all.

As an art form topiary has a universal appeal, partly because there are so many styling options. Whether you consider yourself conservative or traditional, avant garde or eccentric, there is a branch of topiary that is tailor-made for you. One person might add a touch of theatre and grand formality with green architecture, while another will go with the flow and create naturalistic, free-form shapes. With figurative pieces you can introduce a note of quirkiness and humour, while simple geometric forms make serene sculptural additions to modern minimalist landscapes. It does not matter how small your garden is or how ordinary the setting, there is always room for

topiary. It can be grown in pots and some of the tall, slender shapes take up very little room. You do not even need to plant from scratch because existing shrubbery and hedging can often be reshaped and sculpted according to your whim.

Another less obvious factor that draws even novice gardeners to topiary is the sheer pleasure associated with clipping and training something wild and untamed, to create order out of chaos and to see the desired shapes gradually emerging or being further perfected. Neatness freaks beware – this can be an addictive pastime! The fact that architectural elements and statuary can be "constructed" or "sculpted" purely from plants is also something to be marvelled at. Looking at the financial benefits of topiary, provided you have a degree of patience, you can include substantial features such as green walls, archways and colonnades that would cost significantly more to build from dressed stone or bricks and mortar.

The first mention of topiary can be found in the writings of Roman natural historian and scientist Pliny the Elder (AD 62–110) who described fanciful and elaborate elements in his Tuscan garden. Topiary spread far and wide with the advances of the Empire, and some archaeological evidence still remains. At the Roman palace gardens of Fishbourne in Sussex, in England, the pattern of a beautifully ornate box hedge has been revealed.

During the Dark Ages, topiary was still practised but only within monastic gardens and castle defences. The 14th century saw the dawn of the Italian Renaissance, which drew inspiration from classical times and profoundly influenced European garden style. Two of the most beautifully preserved gardens of this period are found at Villa Lante and Villa d'Este, near Rome.

Above Topiarists have always been willing to experiment with different plants, and certain species have risen to peaks of popularity through the ages.

Right A row of lollipop-headed bay standards adds style to this Mediterranean herb garden.

Below No garden is too small for potted topiary.

The formal gardens of the French Renaissance were more imposing, with huge box parterres and avenues lined with hedging that took your eye to some far distant point. Man's dominance over nature was a common theme and master of this style was the architect le Notre who was responsible for the gardens of Vaux le Vicomte, and Louis XIV's Palais de Versailles in the late 17th century. At the same time, topiary and formality had reached America, and from Williamsburg, in Virginia, a simple, ordered style of gardening spread across the colonies.

In Britain, during the Tudor and Elizabethan periods, the knot garden was a popular feature but by the 17th century all manner of curious creatures were also being created in topiary. Meanwhile, in the Netherlands, the passion for topiary was reaching fever pitch and when William of Orange took the throne in Britain in 1688 he introduced a lavish style of formal gardening that was much copied by the isle's wealthiest citizens. Ultimately, the craze for topiary was swept away in a reaction to its excesses and the Landscape Movement went to extraordinary lengths to rid the country of artificiality.

Fashions come and go, and by the 19th century classical formality was beginning to make a comeback. The Victorians created parterres in public parks and gardens and were passionate about colour, filling the patterns with all kinds of vividly coloured bedding plants and exotics.

Above right The vast parterres of Villandry in the Loire Valley, France, comprise hedged compartments filled with colourful flowers and ornamental vegetables.

Right This is the recreation of the original box hedge discovered by archaeologists at the Roman Palace of Fishbourne in West Sussex, in England.

The recent resurgence of interest in topiary can be traced to a number of factors. In the 1960s, American gardeners began developing a form of topiary using wire frames covered in moss and creeping plants, and by the late 1980s this type of portable topiary or "chlorophyll" began to exert an influence across the Atlantic. Appealing to gardeners wanting instant results, chlorophyll is now catching on fast in Europe. Another key reason for topiary's new lease of life was the renewed interest in formality and the desire to recreate authentic period gardens during the 1980s and early 1990s. At this time, a number of high-profile historic garden restorations took place across Britain and Europe, and the gardening public became caught up in a wave of nostalgia. Sales of boxwood soared as parterres, knot gardens and potagers sprang up across Britain, and it was only in the late 1990s that the alarming spread of a new and virulent type of box blight dampened enthusiasm.

Topiary today is more a medium for self-expression than a symbol of status. New modernists, including Piet Oudolf and Jacques Wirtz, have restyled the art to complement contemporary settings, sometimes using a combination of solid

Above Topiary can be used in a range of garden settings, even beside an expanse of water. The geometric shapes of these topiary forms work well next to the fluidity of the pool.

Right Contemporary garden designers increasingly use abstract topiary forms and green architectural elements in order to create visually exciting shapes and textures.

abstract shapes and billowing cloud formations in place of more traditional elements. You only have to look at Jeff Koons' giant "puppy" outside the Guggenheim museum in Bilbao to see just how far things have come. Despite its ancient lineage, topiary is now well and truly established as a 21st-century art form.

This book explores the widest definition of topiary and includes all kinds of shaped greenery, from turf-covered earthworks and green-willow structures to box spirals and yew pyramids. You will find sections on how to incorporate topiary and green architecture, and the different styles that can be created. A wide range of shapes and forms are detailed and the later chapters also include several easy-to-follow, step-by-step projects. The final pages introduce some of the most useful plants for topiary, including which varieties to look out for. Generously illustrated, this is an inspirational sourcebook for anyone interested in adding topiary or green architecture to their garden.

Above Renowned for his perennial plantings, Dutch garden designer Piet Oudolf created this waveform hedge in his garden.

Below Topiary frequently spawns intriguing designs as figures "evolve" or are cut into fanciful shapes, like this abstract elephant.

TOPIARY STYLE

When it comes to choosing a style of topiary for your garden, the age of the house and any significant architectural features can be a useful starting point. Rather than slavishly recreating whole gardens typical of a period, it is usually possible to borrow a little from history. For example, a Victorian garden might well have had an ornate box parterre filled with colourful bedding plants, but if you prefer clean, contemporary lines, you could introduce the required note of formality by laying out simple geometric shapes created from low clipped hedging, highlighted with topiary elements like spheres and cones. The compartments could be filled with aggregates for ease of maintenance.

Inspiration for a topiary garden might come from a holiday destination, illustrations in a book or images from a film. Have you been bowled over by the grandeur of Versailles or the romance of a villa garden in Tuscany? Or, are you more taken with the stylized naturalism of Japanese gardens with clipped azaleas and cloud-pruned pines?

Left This scene demonstrates just how important different topiary styles can be in influencing the mood and character of a garden – in this case, the design harks back to the Italian Renaissance.

Adding one or two signature topiary features to the basic design is often a more workable alternative to making a historically authentic garden. For instance, if you wanted to give a flavour of classical antiquity to a suburban garden, you could flank an entranceway with a pair of large topiary spirals planted in ornate terracotta pots, separate the garden into rooms using tall formal hedges, or line a rectangular pool with perfectly matched box balls.

Many of us now live in modern houses that do not have particularly strong historical links and this frees us to go in any direction we like. A mixture of traditional, geometric topiary figures plus billowing free-form topiary would work well in the surrounds of a simply designed building. But if the house is uninspiring and your garden feels rather flat, you could introduce flamboyant flourishes such as a pleached lime *allée* leading to a bench seat or triple ball standards set into the corners of a square lawn. Quirky elements give a garden an eccentric character, such as training giant turret-shaped topiaries complete with peacock finials on either side of a modest gateway. Lovers of the cottage-garden style might clip chickens and other farmyard creatures. So, whether your approach is contemporary or rooted in history, clipped and trained forms can reinforce the design and create visual drama in a garden that lacks any strong theme or style.

Left A formal layout, with key points emphasized by clipped geometric topiary forms, creates a strong framework that can be filled in with more carefree planting. This approach is ideal for a relaxed country garden attached to a period property.

Right In traditional Japanese gardens, evergreens are often clipped into undulating organic shapes – stylized representations of natural landforms and even cloudscapes. Here, the topiary has the feel of giant, water-worn boulders and makes a wonderful foil for the overhanging black pine.

CHOOSING A STYLE

Classic topiary shapes and structures can create a very different look, depending on how they are combined. Using mixtures of topiary and green architecture with other plants and hard landscaping materials provides endless variations that can alter the character of a garden.

Container-grown topiary is a good example of the way in which clipped shapes can be used to "tweak" the finished look. Box balls in tall, galvanized planters are perfect in a modern, minimalist design. The same plants grown in weathered clay pots enrich the atmosphere of a country garden and when planted up in ornate terracotta or carved stone add drama to a Renaissance-style terrace.

However, you do not have to stick to any "rules" or go for historical accuracy. Topiary can be a useful vehicle for introducing features that technically belong to a different period or style, purely for dramatic effect. There is no reason, for example, why you could not include a parterre in a hi-tech urban courtyard – using brightly coloured glass chips as infill in place of traditional gravel. Why not clip organic, go-with-the-flow greenery around the margins of an old stone fisherman's cottage? This new-style topiary technique can be used to reflect the wild landscape and even capture qualities of the

sea and cloudscape. When developing a formal garden around a period property, you can create the required ambience or look by adding a few key elements of green, structural planting – outlining the edges of lawns and pathways, highlighting changes in level and emphasizing entrances within the garden. The strategic placement of elements such as box balls, cones or spirals makes a truly atmospheric recreation possible.

If no particular style or historical period appeals and you'd prefer to fly in the face of convention, then why not make your garden into a unique artistic statement and expression of your own individuality using elements of green sculpture, as topiary aficionados have been doing for centuries.

Right The grounds of this rambling country manor house are underpinned with a formal plan, the pathways defined and punctuated with softly rendered and repeated topiary cones.

renaissance

The gardens of the Italian and later French Renaissance had a profound effect on gardens in the rest of Europe, with the wealthy, privileged classes creating horticultural extravaganzas designed solely to impress. The stunningly theatrical gardens of Louis XIV at Versailles proclaimed the Sun King's dominance over nature, and were built on a scale designed to dwarf the visitor and leave them filled with a sense of awe.

Today, you can use the same key elements of geometric formality and symmetry and manipulate scale and proportion to trick the eye into imagining the space to be much larger than it really is. The strong structure brings about order in among the chaos of flowers and creates a serene and restful place.

Topiarized shapes, such as sharply pointed pyramids and cones, spheres and domes, columns and colonnades, were used to create rhythm in Renaissance-style gardens and to punctuate, and strengthen, the ground plan. These gardens,

Above Once perfectly balanced and in proportion, these yew pyramids have "drifted" over time, but there's no mistaking the influence of the Renaissance.

Below The grounds of this Florentine villa are laid out as a series of intricate box parterres and wide pathways lined with statuary.

with so much structure and pattern, did not have to rely on colourful blooms for interest. At Renishaw Hall, in Derbyshire, England, Sir George Sitwell used only white blooms to avoid detracting from the green architecture, statuary, pools and fountains when designing his Italianate garden 100 years ago.

In smaller town and city gardens, you could copy and scale down some of the effects seen at Italian jewels like Villa Lante and Palazzo Farnese, using dwarf hedging to divide the space into geometrically shaped compartments containing lawn, gravel or water. Few people have room to reproduce the intricately wrought French-style parterres shown in pattern books of the period, but it is quite easy to create a small-scale copy or plan a simple, repeating border. Certain props such as large Italianate terracotta vases or Versailles planters containing spirals or globe-headed standards make an acceptable substitute for classical statuary, and will give your modest patch a flavour of continental grandeur without breaking the bank.

Above Renaissance gardens relied on formality and symmetry to achieve their effect. Here, a modern interpretation of these principles creates similar results.

Below A stone fountain forms the central focus to a stepped garden relieved by yew topiaries cut to mirror their surroundings.

country house

Topiary is a signature of the classic country garden, the structural elements worked in against a backdrop of billowing herbaceous borders and festooning roses. Though the layout of many period properties is formal, the atmosphere can be surprisingly relaxed. The laid-back ambience of formal gardens is often caused by mature topiary gradually losing its crisp shape; in fact, you are more likely to find grand old holly, yew and holm oak (*Quercus ilex*) figures with generous curves than immaculate angles, even if they started out mirroring the carved stonework of the property.

Alleés of pleached lime or stilt hedges made from hornbeam add a slightly more formal note to a main drive and, on larger properties, giant cylinders or turrets of clipped greenery can be used to create avenues directing the eye towards some distant point, way beyond the ha-ha. But the garden of the country house is ultimately less about show and more about comfort and practicality, exuding a lived-in feeling.

To achieve this, the grounds are often divided into smaller, more intimate areas, each bounded by hedging incorporating an arched entranceway. Within each space, low walls of box

frame an exuberance of summer flowers and herbs, and clipped balls and domes define the intricacies of the ground plan. Knot gardens are rarely cut with the precision reserved for the parterres in a French château, their interweaving threads often being composed of less well-behaved plants than box, such as cotton lavender and shrubby thyme. Immaculate clipping might well look out of place where the stone terraces or brickwork pathways are weathered and uneven.

Above Tulip-filled parterres at Levens Hall in Cumbria add early colour in front of a bizarre collection of aged yew topiary.

Left Though formal in layout, with clipped hedges and box balls providing additional structure, this delightful country garden has a relaxed atmosphere.

Left With the half-timbered wing of the house at the end of this vista, a theatrical stage set has been created to lead the eye and to frame the view.

Below left Quirky topiary figures and hedging finials add character to the country garden. Birds and animals make particularly good subjects.

Below right Reminiscent of the Arts and Crafts movement, this tranquil space, enclosed by green walls, opens out to allow views of the pool garden and rose arbour.

cottage

Some of the most remarkable, eye-catching examples of topiary can be found in cottage-style front gardens. Owners derive immense pride from creating and maintaining unique shapes and figures, some of which are larger than life and dwarf both the house and its pocket-handkerchief garden. Keep a look out on your travels.

Besides the familiar animal line-up of squirrels, cockerels, peacocks and so on, it's easy to spot more eccentric, outrageous and wittier kinds of topiary, with some privet hedges even being turned into steam locomotives or dragons. Other gardens take on a fairy-tale or a child-like quality, adding a Hobbit-style yew house with a pheasant perched on top, or by shaping a large flowering shrub, such as *Viburnum tinus*, into a giant toadstool.

Above This charming little window in a hedge, complete with windowbox, is flanked by two gold-leaved standards. The scene has a homespun feel typical of cottage gardens.

Left Detailed touches, like this niche in the dwarf box edging designed to highlight a pot, are what make gardens special.

Right A thatched arbour forms the focus for this delightful rustic garden which is protected from the elements by a curving beech hedge.

If you want to create a topiary flourish the main entrance is an ideal location. Sometimes you'll see a picket gate flanked by a pair of enormous holly finials that have long since blocked the way in, while a hardy, native, hawthorn hedge is often trained up and over a gate to form an arch.

In traditional gardens a straight, central path, which might be flanked by a neat little dwarf lavender or hyssop hedge, leads to the front porch. Standards trained from cuttings or self-sown seedlings, and planted in simple clay pots or wooden barrels, are often used to embellish the front door. Plants with fragrant flowers or aromatic foliage, such as rosemary, lavender and myrtle, are particular favourites. You might also find potted ivy topiaries on simple frames shaped into hearts or chickens.

Right This strutting cockerel could well have been the model for his topiary lookalike marking the entrance to the hen house.

japanese

Traditional Japanese gardens are stylized, scaled-down recreations of the natural landscape, and might include mini mountain ranges, waterfalls, forests, lakes and islands. Colour is restricted to brief seasonal bursts, with a background continuity of green in all its many shades.

Trees and shrubs are often clipped and trained to appear ancient and weather-beaten since age is equated to wisdom. Luxuriant carpets of moss colonize the shady areas, and the preference for evergreens and the way the stepping-stones and rocks are set deep into the ground adds to the atmosphere of peace and stability that is perfect for contemplation.

In larger gardens, you might find a cloud-pruned pine arcing over a pool, but, in the *karesansui* style – which is commonly associated with Zen – water (the *yin* element) is represented by raked gravel, pebbles and cobbles, with "islands" created from rock groupings (the *yang* element). The harmony and balance created between these two opposites is critical. In naturalistic gardens, the ground surrounding the gravel may be contoured with billowing organic forms clipped from evergreen shrubs,

such as azalea, Japanese holly (*Ilex crenata*) and box. Cut into a bank or hillside it's worth including a rocky cascade, the flow suggested by a flat, vertical rock called the water falling stone.

The Japanese excel at miniaturizing and there's no reason why you couldn't convert a tiny back yard into a garden using bamboo screens, rocks, gravel and cloud-pruned trees in pots.

Above This Zen garden in the *karesansui* style contains a sea of pebbles, with mossy hummocks and evergreen shrubs backed by rounded boulders which represent a mountainous interior and lowland plain.

Left Characterful Japanese black pine (*Pinus thunbergii*) help to suggest a wild mountainous landscape and, to complete the picture, evergreens clipped into organic shapes symbolize rock-strewn ground.

Above Hanging over the water, this cloud-pruned tree, which is apparently growing out of a rocky crevice, adds a sense of timelessness to the scene, its shape reminiscent of an aged, wind-blasted pine.

Left Though the cloud pruning here is quite stylized, the rock-like solidity and natural form of the shapes contrast perfectly with the curving roof line and "forest" of bamboo.

courtyard

With the right plants, décor and a bubbling fountain, a bare courtyard of bricks and concrete can be transformed into an oasis of greenery. Geometric pieces of topiary act like sculpted stone and, in a space dominated by the surrounding architecture, make a wonderfully bold, theatrical statement.

If the ground is concrete then topiary must be containerized and most species, with the exception of yew, can be successfully kept in pots. Choose containers to strengthen your design, using anything from traditional, Italianate terracotta to galvanized metal. While the light in a courtyard may be a limiting factor, many plants, including box, ivy and holly, will thrive in shade. And because of the extra shelter, you may also be able to keep more tender plants outdoors all year round.

Below A formal courtyard, with box hedging and clipped box standards in terracotta pots, is a study in elegant simplicity

A matching pair of potted topiaries is ideal for highlighting an entrance, and groups of diverse shapes, including swirling spirals, lollipop-headed standards, stylized birds, balls and cones, are perfect for decorating awkward corners. Also try combining them with pots of annual flowers and bulbs for seasonal highlights, or add a few elegant flowering standards, such as fuchsias, abutilons or marguerite daisies.

Water is an essential ingredient for a courtyard garden. Semi-circular, raised-wall pools are ideal where space is limited but a central pool evokes a blissful atmosphere of tranquillity. Enclose it within low clipped hedging or outline it with dwarf box balls in identical pots. Make the most of limited space by growing upwards and covering bare walls. Ivy can be trained to cover shaped trellis panels or rope swags, the latter creating a sense of rhythm around your outdoor room. Espalier-trained shrubs like firethorn (*Pyracantha*) are also effective and take up little room.

Above This courtyard garden relies heavily on the contrasting shapes and textures of potted topiary for its effect. The golden sphere at the top of the fountain echoes the clipped topiary balls.

Above Potted topiary columns and standards can be placed around a terrace or courtyard in order to create height and drama.

Below The bold symmetry of this beautifully planted walled garden is emphasized by the large golden cones and their tiny potted replicas.

modern classics

The architectural and almost machine-made qualities of some geometric pieces of topiary make them ideally suited for use in modern minimalist landscapes, which often have a rectilinear ground plan. The resulting simplicity of such a design generates a soothing ambience.

Domes, spheres, pyramids, cones and blocks are typically used in contemporary gardens, clipped evergreens usually taking precedence over more colourful annual or perennial blooms, and the palette is restricted mainly to shades of green with perhaps touches of grey or bronze. Interesting combinations of topiary elements include neat evergreen groundcover, ornamental grasses and sculptural plants such as phormiums and yuccas. Two of the hallmarks of contemporary landscaping are purity of line and a sense of space, so it is vital that topiary and green architecture, such as formal hedges, are arranged with sensitivity, particularly with regard to scale and proportion. "Less is more" is an extremely useful guide.

Still pools and other reflective surfaces, including glass and polished metal, can be effectively employed in order to enhance the modern topiary garden in the daytime, while at night spotlights, and even coloured floodlights, can provide drama and excitement.

Sometimes topiary is used like a piece of stone sculpture to create the focal point at the end of a vista, but asymmetry is more usual and it is the mathematical forms, the lines and angles that intrigue. Cloud topiary has also become fashionable for adding a touch of urban chic to city gardens and roof terraces.

Left A carefully composed combination of clipped green walls and sculptural geometric forms, including potted spheres, enlivens this simple space with texture.

Right This highly original architectural garden uses clipped greenery to create a pleasing array of shapes and textures such as the box square filled with cotton lavender (*Santolina*).

Above The reflections in the still pools enhance this simply structured garden of modern formality. Note how the box squares echo the shape of the trellis panels against the wall.

Above This asymmetric yet balanced arrangement of topiary forms made from contrasting materials is the perfect complement for the contemporary building and creates an atmosphere of tranquillity.

new wave

One of the most radical developments in topiary in recent years has been the use of free-flowing, organic shapes. This style of naturalistic contouring is striking when contrasted with crisp architectural elements, such as hedges, formal pools and the walls of buildings, and it also works well as textured groundcover in more relaxed or less intensively cultivated areas of the garden.

The influence of the East is apparent in the billowing, cloud-like forms and this style of clipping is highly adaptable. You can have great fun experimenting, seeing what shapes emerge, and if you have a mature and perhaps slightly overgrown shrub border or unruly mixed hedge you could begin clipping right away. But to achieve a more uniform look in terms of texture and colour, it is advisable to start from scratch by planting in blocks using just one subject such as box.

Plants can also be clipped separately, producing something resembling a basket of eggs, but it is more usual to allow them to fuse, creating an undulating surface of miniature hills and valleys. New wave topiarists also specialize in hedges, screens and other 3-D structures with an abstract profile. Although the shapes may be quite stylized, inspiration for this art form is often derived from the natural world – from waves, snail spirals and curling tendrils, for example.

Another exciting development, which can be traced back to the Land Art Movement of the 1960s, is the contouring of the ground to make turf-covered earthworks. These usually look most effective in large, open areas, and the designs are often symbolic or in some way reflect, or are sympathetic to, the surrounding landscape. The shapes may be fluid and dynamic, such as a single serpentine ridge or a series of wave-like undulations, and, in early morning light or around sunset, the shadows highlight the topography to create a magical effect. More static, geometric landforms suit minimalist, rectilinear designs.

Allied to Land Art but based on ancient symbols, turf labyrinths have also become popular features of New Age gardens. And low hedges laid out to form abstract designs are increasingly used to texture and pattern the ground.

Left Here, the pool margins undulate with clipped box and ivy, while the rounded forms are mirrored on the balcony. Such a free-flowing topiary style is perfect for this setting, cocooning the minimalist architecture.

Above left Mixing traditional and avant-garde elements can be highly effective in garden design. Here, classic standards are set against a striking contemporary backdrop.

Above right The gentle moulding of the ground creates a feeling of enclosure in this small sitting area and the overall design has an abstract simplicity.

Left In this modern interpretation of a parterre with its arcs of clipped box alternating with coloured stone chippings, a blank garden space is transformed.

eccentric

With topiary you can be as conventional or as eccentric as you like. In fact it is often easier, and much more fun, to follow your own surreal ideas than to slavishly copy yet another bird or obelisk. And if figures are non-representational, no one can complain that something doesn't look right.

There seems to be no limit to the subjects that people will attempt, from a man-eating shark clipped from a suburban privet hedge to a fire-breathing dragon or "Nessie" emerging from the Loch. Green Animals, on Rhode Island, USA, has an impressive menagerie of 21 creatures, including a life-size giraffe, elephant, bear and camel. Such shapes turn heads quickly enough, being inherently bizarre, but even more so when they are used in ordinary gardens where they are the last thing that you'd expect to see. Animals are not the only shapes to catch the eye. You could make a giant chess set or tea cup.

Established topiary tends to evolve, drift or get middle-aged spread so that the original outline becomes distorted. At Levens Hall, in Cumbria, England, one tiered figure now leans at

a jaunty angle. Old yew and box hedges are sometimes clipped to follow their natural growth pattern, producing strange eruptions, but in some historic gardens the unique hedge shapes are more deliberate, although their origins have long since been forgotten.

Left Lurking in the shadows, a dragon made from clipped box breathes smoke – or, in actual fact, steam – from its nostrils.

Right Topiary tends to "drift" and evolve over time. At Levens Hall in Cumbria, England, the collection of shapes includes some particularly eccentric examples, such as this cake stand with wobbly tiers, which now leans at a drunken angle.

Below At Walt Disney World, in Florida, a giant *Podocarpus* serpent, like a cartoon Loch Ness monster, appears to be swimming through the water.

DESIGNING WITH TOPIARY

Topiary is an incredibly versatile medium, being invaluable for helping to create the structure of the garden as well as adding decorative sculptural elements and other fun shapes that do not appear in nature. The contrast between the artificiality of topiary and the surrounding natural forms of the garden is central to its appeal. Depending on your approach, results can be theatrical and dramatic, or flowing and organic, the clipped greenery catching the light and often producing dramatic shadows that enliven the atmosphere of the garden. When combined with reflecting pools or sparkling fountains, the effects can be quite magical.

Topiary can also be used to create patterns and designs of varying complexity, to set up pleasing visual rhythms and highlight existing features. You can even use topiary to produce a sense of depth and perspective, and in small or awkwardly shaped plots to create the illusion that the space is much larger than it really is.

Left These magnificent yew pyramids make an imposing feature in this formal garden, and have the look of fortifications, visually strengthening the boundary wall.

Geometric topiary pieces act just like bricks and mortar or carved stonework. Although these elements have a man-made feel, they are far more in keeping in the garden than masonry and so can be used generously without fear of making the space feel lifeless. Some gardens rely entirely on 3-D topiary structures and ground patterns but most strike a balance between the solid clipped figures and the untamed flowers and foliage plants.

Green architecture creates verdant garden rooms and discrete areas of particular character or function such as a terrace, pool garden or vegetable plot. Used skilfully it can manipulate our perception of the space surrounding the house, leading the unwitting visitor through a maze of interconnecting pathways. Directing the eye, you can create vistas and sight lines that lead to particular focal points within the plot or to views outside its boundaries, at the same time blocking off unpleasant or distracting aspects. And continuing in a theatrical vein, archways and tunnels create a frisson of excitement as you pass from one garden room to the next and window-like apertures allow tantalizing glimpses of features on the other side of the screen.

The following pages talk you through some of the main design principles regarding the use of topiary and green architecture, and will help you to plan out your garden or the elements within it.

Left In a relaxed country garden, a low round of box hedging contains an exuberance of summer flowers. The underlying structure of the garden is clearly visible in winter, outlined by topiary and hedging.

Right A long, narrow box parterre, dressed with cones and spheres, runs between a formal hedge and a brick pathway and, despite having only a scattering of blooms, transforms this quiet backwater by way of pleasing shapes.

Far left Formal yew hedging encloses sections of the garden and at key points is clipped into substantial pillars.

Left Here, the clever use of box-edged compartments and luxuriant wall planting eases the transition between house and garden.

FORM AND FUNCTION

Garden design is a combination of aesthetics and practicality; in other words we want the space to look beautiful but we also want it to have a satisfactory structure. One of the key tools for achieving both aims is green architecture – topiary and hedging.

Living architecture includes walls, pillars, arches and entranceways as well as sculpture. These elements literally grow up from the lines of the ground plan and help define the limits and functions of different areas within the garden, as well as providing privacy. Without them, gardens can seem flat and featureless, far too open and lacking depth and textural contrast. This is especially true in winter when the majority of taller, structural herbaceous plants and climbers have died back down to ground level, and the deciduous shrubs have lost their leaves.

Even relatively relaxed, informal plots, which rely heavily on flower and foliage colour, can benefit from a few strategically placed pieces of topiary. The classic cottage garden is a particularly good example. Typically, it has borders to either side of a central path, filled with a seemingly haphazard mix of flowers, herbs and vegetables, but adding a few topiarized shrubs (possibly including an arched entrance of trained greenery) provides an overall shape or pattern and links different elements of the plot together. Evergreens, such as holly and yew, are clipped into simple shapes within borders, while paths and flower beds may be framed with dwarf hedging of lavender or box to frame the exuberant planting behind, making the space feel less "busy".

In formal designs, a large proportion of the "bones" of the garden may be fashioned from topiary, but this technique isn't restricted to traditional garden styles or the grounds of period properties. Many contemporary designers incorporate geometric topiary pieces and formal hedging into minimalist or avant-garde spaces where the look relies on clean lines and solid, well-defined shapes contrasting with open spaces or voids in the form of lawns, pools or paving.

Right The view down into this cool, leafy courtyard is enhanced by the bold ground pattern.

outlining

In a garden with a formal or geometric layout, the shapes and patterns created by the ground plan, as well as any changes in level, can be highlighted and enhanced by strategically placed pieces of topiary and low-level hedging.

Low, clipped, evergreen hedges of box, Japanese holly (*Ilex crenata*), Yaupon holly (*Ilex vomitoria*), santolina and lavender and, for variegated foliage, cultivars of *Euonymus fortunei*, can be used to frame and delineate a wide range of features.

The results can be particularly effective when the borders are bare (in winter, for example, or having only been recently planted), and it only takes a couple of years for the plants of the new hedge to merge into a respectable, shapely line. Use topiary to outline paths and sections of paving, areas of coloured gravel, formal pools and lawns. If you wish to add decorative detail to a kitchen garden, why not create a potager with several separate beds, all framed by low evergreen hedging?

Above This grand stairway is given greater prominence by yew and box cut to resemble carved stone.

Where two paths converge, creating a mini cross roads, you can highlight the junction by marking the corners with matching pieces of topiary, such as small pyramids or dome-shaped finials. These can be set into the right-angled spaces or be cut from the hedge itself.

Matching pieces of topiary can also be used to highlight changes in level, for example at the top and bottom of a flight of steps. Whether planted in pots or set in the ground, they can also be used to mark the transition from one area of the garden to another, such as from the terrace to the ornamental lawn and flower borders and from there to the vegetable plot or wild area. Tall slim shapes, such as cypress columns, Irish yew flasks and slender yew pyramids, make wonderful exclamation marks and, when planted equidistantly in long rows, can be used to form an *alleé*. The same plants could also be arranged to form a semicircular *exedra*, perhaps highlighting the arc of a formal pool.

Above Set into a leaf-strewn lawn, either side of a long, straight pathway, matching rows of box spheres and cones guide the visitor to the front door.

Above Picking up on the ball-shaped stone finials on top of the gate posts, golden *Euonymus japonicus* standards, surrounded by neat box hedging, enhance this formal gateway.

Left Beyond the box cones and sundial centrepiece, tall yew cylinders form a much narrower passageway, hiding the rest of the garden and creating an atmosphere of mystery and intrigue.

entrances

Topiary and forms of green architecture are often used to define and enhance doors, gates and entrances in boundaries as well as internal divisions being used to separate different parts of the garden.

One simple idea is to set a matching pair of potted topiary pieces either side of the front door. Traditional selections for a year-round display include box balls and spirals, and lollipop-headed standards of box, holly, bay, privet (*Ligustrum delavayanum*) and, in mild areas, myrtle. It is most important to select your sentinels carefully because any difference in height, shape or stature will be immediately apparent. Holly and bay standards are useful for larger entrances because the stems can be grown to a greater height without requiring staking. For flowers by the door, try *Viburnum tinus*, camellia, cultivars of *Hydrangea paniculata* or, in very mild regions, *Leptospermum scoparium*. You should also make sure that you turn potted topiary around on a regular basis to prevent the side next to the wall becoming threadbare through lack of light.

Around doors, growing plants such as yew, holly, holm oak (*Quercus ilex*), pyracantha and hornbeam in the ground instead of in containers, gives the potential for creating large architectural structures. You might consider growing a porch or arch where an entrance needs more prominence, or training a pair of free-standing columns, clipped pillars or buttresses.

Above Although this classically inspired veranda is actually just a clever *trompe l'oeil*, the illusion of depth is enhanced by placing box cones at the entranceway.

Left Acting like stone fortifications, these impressive yew turrets, which are not quite a matching pair, mark the transition from the formal garden to the semi-wild surrounding landscape.

When gates are set in a formal hedge, add greater weight and importance to the entrance by sculpting and training the adjacent hedging to resemble posts, perhaps topped with finials, or shaped walling with wings rising up on either side. Gateposts should be well defined and can be clipped to extend outwards, well beyond the face of the hedge, even forming large cylinders or turrets. Another way of making evergreen pillars and posts prominent is by using contrasting foliage, for example golden holly, set against a dark green holly hedge.

When developing entrances, it is fun to opt for larger-than-life features that verge on the grandiose. Try training the hedge to resemble a stonework arch even if the gate is modest, and instead of ball- or pyramid-shaped finials, try a pair of cake stands, stylized peacocks or even heraldic eagles for a touch of theatre.

Right It is not difficult to train more vigorous plants such as beech or conifer hedging into archways.

Below Tapering yew columns emphasize this simple metal bridge.

Below right The foliage around the acorn finial is carefully trimmed to maintain it as an integral feature of the hedge.

juxtaposition

There is a great deal to be gained from exploring the relationship between the natural and artificial. In a formal plot, it can be intriguing to effect marked contrasts by juxtaposing perfectly clipped shapes, including hedges and screens, with completely untamed areas.

If your garden borders the countryside, there's likely to be ample opportunity for some theatrical stage setting. You might, for example, place a line of topiarized figures along the boundary line or clip a hedge with finials to create a clearly defined break between the man-made garden and the wild or agricultural scenery beyond. One of the best examples of such a dramatic contrast can be seen when looking down from the upper terraces of Mapperton Gardens, in Dorset, England.

From this vantage point you see, laid out clearly below, the formal valley garden with large topiary pieces surrounding a long rectangular pool. As the land rises again, there is apparently no boundary between this highly architectural set piece and the backdrop of rolling hills, a perfect example of borrowed landscape. Another factor in the success of Mapperton is that the dark yew figures that line the pool garden echo the shapes of the surrounding wild trees.

In a large plot you might have space for a wild garden seeded with native species. Although sinuous mown paths can create quite a pleasing contrast, you could add more structure and interest to the scene by bordering the garden with a dark formal hedge such as yew. This would also act as a matt backdrop to enhance the display of blooms and seed heads. Alternatively, try placing two or three large topiary figures in the long grass, keeping the turf clear of the base. Suitable

Above In winter, the relationship between an eccentric grouping of box figures and the woodland backdrop is intriguing.

Left Nature versus nurture – this wildflower meadow is backed by a clipped yew hedge with topiary finials.

subjects include stylized birds and animals, but abstract or geometric shapes work equally effectively in gardens with a contemporary feel.

To mark the transition from one style of garden room to another – leading from the ornamental garden, for example, into the fruit and vegetable plot – try ornate entrances cut through formal hedging, or perhaps mock topiary gateposts lining a pathway. These features are reminiscent of old mansion houses with their walled gardens, and can elevate an ordinary suburban plot into something special by giving it a touch of unexpected grandeur.

Left Naturalized cyclamen add a carefree note but man's gardening activities are evident in the nearby topiary avenue.

Below The rolling hills in the distance provide the perfect canvas for the pool garden at Mapperton, in Dorset, England.

creating depth

Topiary and elements of green architecture, such as hedges and colonnades, can be used to frame views with layer upon layer of structure. The process can be likened to composing a picture or designing a stage set where the aim is to create a sense of depth even in a relatively small space.

It is easier to play around with perspective when you have an asymmetrical layout instead of one built around a central axis, for example. By overlaying contrasting shapes and blocks to create foreground, middle distant and far distant focal points, you can develop lines of perspective and perhaps even take the view beyond the limits of the garden. This technique of borrowed landscape, or *shakkei* as it is known in Japan, relies on the boundaries being camouflaged or blurred so that the surrounding countryside or a chosen feature (a beautiful old tree or church spire, for example) appears to be part of the garden. This trick can greatly increase the perceived size of the plot, as well as making the outlook far more interesting.

Another way to deceive the eye and create false perspective is to repeat the same profile, such as a pyramid, at key points. The shapes closest to the onlooker are grown and trained to be the largest, and progressively decrease in size towards the margins of the garden. You could employ a similar technique in a garden with a central pathway, when it is often more effective to partially obscure the view at intervals so that the garden unfolds gradually as you move forward.

At the late Piet Bekaert's garden, in the middle of the Belgian countryside, the artist's house, a striking piece of modern architecture, sits at the centre of a visually arresting geometrical framework. An extraordinary array of elements is used, including pools, a pergola, hedges, topiary, trees and clipped, organic forms. They combine to create a texturally rich green garden with tantalizing glimpses of the surrounding fields. The garden relies almost entirely on perspective and the interaction of different forms instead of flower colour.

Above Crisp hedging screens placed either side of the pathway act like pieces of scenery on a stage set, preventing the eye from rushing to the end.

Above These tall yew pyramids really emphasize the lines of perspective in the garden, appearing to get smaller towards the end of the pathway.

Above Laying out different sizes and shapes of topiary and using a mixture of evergreen and golden foliage makes the garden seem deeper.

Left This clever banking and multi-layering of topiary elements and hedging creates a sense of depth in the short space between the house and the boundary.

mirroring

Topiary is such a versatile medium that you can copy or mimic the shapes of all kinds of architectural or sculptural features. The aim is to grab the visitor's attention with something witty or beautiful, and possibly lead the eye on to other important features in the garden.

Elements worth copying include eccentric or ornate chimneys, finials on gateposts, and garden sculptures, obelisks or vases. A nearby building or surrounding wall might also be worth echoing in clipped greenery, producing castellations in a hedge, or a series of archways or colonnades cut out of a screen of × *Cupressocyparis leylandii*.

Historic houses, or ones with period detail, often have unique features which can be picked out. For example, Gothic arched windows might appear first in the main building, again in the summerhouse or gazebo, and finally in the boundary hedges giving views across surrounding fields. Patterns are also worth copying, and you could reproduce the diamond design

Above Fastigiate yews, cleverly clipped to mirror the elegant curves of these bow-fronted figures, stand out against the autumn leaves of this beech hedge.

Below At the atmospheric Elsing Hall in Norfolk, England, a gathering of no fewer than 64 yew pyramids surrounds an obelisk to theatrical effect.

Above A monkey carved in stone sits facing its replica clipped freehand from box.

of leaded windows, *treillage* panels or brickwork in a simple parterre, or by decorating a wall with a criss-cross of English ivy (*Hedera helix*). It can be a touch of whimsy to echo the exact image of a sculpture opposite or even right next to it. There are two ways of going about this. The easiest is to commission a 3-D metal frame so that you don't have to worry about getting the shapes and proportions right but, if you are reasonably confident, just get snipping. It's rarely possible to cut the whole piece in one go. Do it in stages, and allow the plant to recover and grow between sessions.

Mirroring doesn't have to be exact, and it is sometimes only possible to reproduce a rough copy of the object or feature, perhaps scaled down. However, the closer you get to a precise copy, the better. Modern architecture also provides scope for mirroring. Beside an A-frame house, for example, you could train a series of giant pyramids in yew, beech or hornbeam with exactly the same angle at the apex. And a geodesic-dome greenhouse could spawn a surreal landscape of clipped forms. In a country garden, a beekeeper might even add some beehives or old-fashioned skeps snipped from box.

Above Topiary and green architecture often reflect the shapes of nearby buildings and here the similarity between the yew pyramids and tiled roof is clearly evident.

Below Like giant chess pieces, these box topiary figures sit on either side of the original stone model.

emphasis

Clipped foliage can create the same impression as dressed stone or bricks and mortar. It combines very easily with existing architecture, and can also help to strengthen or develop certain shapes and give features, such as entrances, greater weight and substance. So, if you have grand design ideas as well as dramatic flair, but only limited funds, all you need is patience and a pair of shears.

Wildly theatrical examples of augmenting architecture are evident in grander gardens. In one a façade built to resemble the entrance to an ancient tomb was made even more imposing by soaring walls of yew "stonework" and evergreen "Egyptian" pyramids. Translating this approach to a domestic setting, instead of building an elegant porch over the front door, why not grow one using hornbeam or yew trained over a metal or wooden framework?

Along the garden boundary, low walls can be increased in size, height and stature by growing a hedge behind them. This can then be trained over the top and clipped to give a smooth, parallel face. Alternatively, you could overhang the wall and clip the hedge with a curved profile like a roll-top desk.

Further embellishments to add to a formal hedge-wall combination might include evergreen finials. In a more relaxed setting you might consider shaping the top of the hedge in an undulating fashion. If you are starting the design from scratch, you could also build a wall which has regularly spaced brick piers, filling the spaces between them with formal hedging. You can then cut the top of the hedge level with the piers or into curves which dip down between the brick columns.

Above The shape of these slender finials would be lost were it not for the dark yew backdrop.

Left In order to augment a low wall, the foreground of yew hedging has been clipped to resemble stonework.

Architectural balance can sometimes be achieved using topiary to supply missing elements. At Arley Hall, in Cheshire, England, substantial yew buttresses, with a stepped and curving profile, "support" a red brick wall. The opposite wall of yew hedging mirrors the structure perfectly, and the two sides make the ideal backdrop for a double herbaceous border. On a smaller scale, you could embellish a structure, such as a plain wooden bench by converting it into a Lutyens-style seat with scrolled armrests.

Above *Faux* buttresses in yew appear to support this brick wall and add substance to the herbaceous planting.

Right Mixed hollies, clipped to overhang this wall, strengthen the barrier that holds back the looming yew trees.

textural contrast

One of the most exciting aspects of designing with topiary and green architecture is the way in which you can make the most of the difference between natural, untrained elements and those artistically clipped forms created by the gardener.

Unless the plot has a clean-lined, minimalist layout, there is always going to be a contrast between the clipped greenery and the somewhat chaotic form of flowers and foliage. A particularly pleasing combination involves a formal hedge that is overhung by the branches of a tree or large, flowering shrub. When a dark, fine-grained hedge, such as yew, forms the backdrop to a traditional herbaceous border, the green "wall" makes a perfect foil to highlight the intricate detail of bloom and leaf. At Elvaston Castle, in Derbyshire, England, there is a different kind of contrast. Several pieces of topiary are clipped in a bizarre, half-and-half manner. This came about quite by accident when the gardeners discovered that their ladders only reached part-way up the giant, golden yews. For safety's sake, the higher portions were left to grow naturally with the branches like flickering flames shooting out of the top of the plants.

Many people begin practising topiary without realizing it, smartening up certain shrubs by snipping them into ball or dome shapes. Sometimes, natural, irregular growth suggests another shape, such as an animal or cloud, which can then be accentuated. The trick is knowing when to stop clipping, otherwise you can end up with a garden full of curiosities where all the shrubs, no matter how inappropriately, are trained into characterless "blobs". With bare ground in between, there is no relief from the visual monotony.

Small-leaved evergreens are ideal for clipping, especially those with a dense, rounded, cone-shaped or columnar profile. Examples of suitable shrubs which are commonly found in mixed borders include *Euonymus fortunei* and cultivars of *E. japonicus*; hollies; many small-leaved hebes; lavenders and cotton lavenders; *Osmanthus* x *burkwoodii*; *Lonicera nitida* 'Baggesen's Gold'; and small-leaved cotoneasters.

When the borders contain a good balance between solid topiary and loose, free-flowing shapes, the results are texturally rich and exciting. Colour is almost secondary, and it is a good idea to try to visualize the scene in black and white when planning seasonal and herbaceous planting to accompany topiary. Bold architectural plants can be effective teamed with rounded forms, but diaphanous flowers and feathery foliage make topiary shapes appear even more like carved stone.

Left Lavender fills the spaces between this immaculately clipped *parterre de broderie*, thereby accentuating the stone-like quality of the box topiary.

Right Around this swirling parterre in the grounds of Elvaston Castle, in Derbyshire, England, the contrast between the clipped segments of golden yew and the parts that have been left to grow naturally is very striking.

Above Clipping this specimen of *Euonymus fortunei* 'Silver Queen' has enhanced the contrast between the surrounding plants.

Above An identically clipped grouping of hebe spheres, teamed with a statuesque New Zealand flax (*Phormium tenax*) for a strong vertical accent, adds a contemporary note to this mixed border.

GROUND PATTERN

Some of the most effective forms of topiary involve texturing the ground surface using mathematical curves, spirals and other classic geometric shapes in order to create a varied, lively background. Very often, these shapes are best viewed from an elevated vantage point.

The chequerboard design of solid green squares alternating with paving or gravel is sometimes seen in Japanese Zen gardens where trimmed moss is used, but you could clip any number of woody evergreens to create this pattern. The green-on-green of open box rectangles set in a lawn relies entirely on light and shade to highlight and define the shapes. Such simple forms, though effective, are far removed from the flamboyant *parterre de broderie* of a French château. In a contemporary setting, a collection of identically potted plants can be attractively displayed by setting them out on a chequerboard of paving squares separated by gravel or placed in sockets cut into the centres of green topiary blocks. Developing the square theme further, try a Greek key motif as a border around a plain feature, such as a rectangular pool.

More free-flowing, complex topiarized shapes, such as precision-cut, flat-topped curls and spirals, tend to work best with a contrasting backdrop such as fine grit or gravel, coloured stone chippings or chipped glass. But where the topiary design is congested, ground cover is rarely necessary. For example, at Château de Breteuil, near Paris, a shady bank showcases a living mosaic of box plants clipped into multifaceted shapes. Here, groundcover is redundant.

The basket-of-eggs effect is quite easy to create using clipped domes or spheres, and some plants naturally develop the required habit with very little training. These include cotton lavender (*Santolina chamaecyparissus* and *S. rosmarinifolia* subsp. *rosmarinifolia*), cultivars of English lavender (*Lavandula angustifolia*) and small-leaved hebes (such as *Hebe* 'Red Edge', *H. topiaria* and *H. rakaiensis*). Because the design is modular, this pattern is useful for filling irregular spaces.

the view from above

The best view of a ground pattern is to be had from a raised vantage point. The complex, intertwining knots created by the Elizabethans were often set out beneath the long gallery on the upper floor of a manor house where they could be admired from the windows. And in the grand gardens of the French and Italian Renaissance period, the vast, intricately wrought parterres were viewed from elevated terraces and walkways.

Looking down into a garden from above gives a completely different perspective, and it can be fun to create a surprise for visitors by designing patterns or symbols which only become apparent from a certain angle. The tower at the centre of

Sissinghurst Castle Gardens, in Kent, England, provides a novel way of appreciating the formal layout, and this inspired the Irish designer Jim Reynolds to build a smaller version at his own Butterstream garden, in County Meath, Ireland, so that people could view the parterre below.

In a modern city or suburban location, you might create a ground pattern to enjoy from a bedroom window or first floor office. Front gardens can appear quite plain and functional when looked down on, but you could enliven a featureless, gravel parking area with a small knot or parterre, or use this idea to create an attractive, low maintenance feature to replace a tiny lawn which is inconvenient to mow.

Patterns don't have to be symmetrical. Instead, you could simply create a series of pleasing shapes like an island chain seen from the air, a beautiful French curve or long-tailed spiral. Or, for a contemporary site, try setting out widely spaced clipped spheres or cones in a square grid pattern, either planted in the ground or potted in galvanized containers.

A view on to a grassy bank or slope can be transformed by creating shapes with low, clipped, evergreen hedging, and filling in with contrasting materials. For a sunny site, you could use *Ilex crenata* 'Golden Gem' and, in the centre, the dwarf lavender, *Lavandula angustifolia* 'Hidcote'; in shade, try a dwarf box such as *Buxus microphylla* 'Faulkner' filled with green-and-white variegated *Euonymus fortunei* 'Emerald Gaiety' clipped to the same height. For a shallow bank, try carving patterns into closely mown turf, historically referred to as "grasswork in the English manner".

Left In a garden in London's suburbia, a long, narrow knot garden, with a diamond-shaped design, enhances the views from the upstairs windows.

Right The extensive parterres at Château de Villandry, in France, come in a dazzling array of patterns, the designs accentuated by plantings of brightly coloured bedding.

Above To best appreciate the swirling and often complex patterns of a parterre, you really need an elevated vantage point, whether this is an upstairs window or a raised terrace area.

Above This design, resembling the spokes of a wheel, could easily be accommodated in a small garden, perhaps viewed from a deck or balcony. Fill the spaces with bedding or herbs.

rhythm and repetition

The eye is drawn to regularly spaced, repeated elements and man-made features stand out clearly against the softer backdrop of foliage and flowers. A row of equidistantly positioned shapes, such as topiarized columns, clipped standards, balls and domes, sets up a rhythm or tempo in the garden, making the space feel more dynamic. It's rather like applying a decorative border in interior design work, or fixing swags of fabric to dress a window. In fact, ivy can be used to create festoons, linking identical elements together in a continuous, looping line. Such features help create a sense of movement, enlivening an outdoor space which feels too static while, perhaps, leading the eye towards a focal point. Tree-lined avenues are a classic example, and you see many variations in the grounds of stately homes or country manor houses, some using pleached screens, others tall, clipped cylinders.

A variety of different hedging styles can also be employed to establish a rhythm, for example, along with piers or buttresses, a scalloped top or regularly spaced clipped finials. Raised or stilt hedges and colonnades have the same effect, the trunks or columns tapping out a regular beat. Hedges can also be cut with regularly spaced alcoves or vertical grooves.

To give a herbaceous or mixed border more substance, and to create a pleasing structure, try planting a line of obelisks or ball-headed standards along the length. Fastigiate yews and other conifers, including Italian cypress and certain junipers, produce a similar effect with less need for training.

Below A continuous line of stilt hedging forms a border around this sunken feature whose design is highlighted with box balls. The repetition of the balls has a soothing effect on the viewer.

Above A repeating pattern of box hedging cut with square apertures and cone-shaped finials is augmented by holly standards.

Above Santolina balls laid out with geometric precision make an eye-catching feature dotted with purple tripods.

Below Yew obelisks, arranged neatly to create a wide avenue, echo the pointed roof of the building in the distance.

LIGHT AND SHADE

Natural light works a particular kind of magic on topiary gardens and, on a bright day, when the shadows are well-defined and the lit faces of clipped greenery gleam in the sunlight, the shapes can be properly appreciated. At different times of day subtle changes in light occur.

Undulating organic forms and the weaving strands of a knot garden are most beautifully illuminated in early morning and towards sundown when the slanting light brings out the subtleties of their contouring. This applies not only to clipped greenery but also to turf-covered earthworks including labyrinths. Meanwhile, in summer, at around midday, when the contrast between light and shadow is most well defined, substantial geometric topiary shapes, such as pyramids and tiered cake stands, as well as swirling *parterres de broderie*, take on the qualities of carved stonework.

Gardens are enlivened by contrast. In the summer, moving from starkly lit open areas to the dappled shade of an *allée* that is bordered by pleached lime or perhaps the cool interior of a laburnum arch or yew tunnel is utterly blissful. Too much shade in the garden is a problem, however, and an outdoor space that is overshadowed by large trees or buildings can often feel dull and claustrophobic. Such a situation might be remedied by introducing an open area such as a pool or perhaps a formal lawn that is outlined with low, clipped hedging or even a small knot garden filled with pale, light-reflecting gravel.

When backlit, topiary shapes and elements of green architecture throw wonderful shadow patterns onto the ground, and in formal gardens in particular, the rhythm of repeated forms, such as a row of ball-headed standards or the stems of a stilt hedge, is reinforced.

Above left Grouping contrasting topiary forms together produces complex shadow patterns that enhance shape and texture.

Above right When light shines onto a stilt hedge, it creates a pleasing rhythmic pattern of shadows.

Right At certain times of day, geometric shapes like these impressive yew pyramids come into sharp relief.

shadow patterns

One of the unexpected bonuses of adding sculptural and architectural elements to the garden is the way that they create all kinds of shadowy shapes and patterns on the ground, and even on vertical surfaces.

With the light behind them, sharply defined pieces of topiary act like 2-D templates creating intriguingly shaped shadows which, depending on the season or time of day, will be long or short, precise or strangely distorted. The effect is particularly important during the winter months when the landscape is stripped to its bare bones. On a crisp, blue-sky day, all the contoured shapes and geometric structures are doubled by their negative images. That is a very good reason for making sure that the topiary has been well clipped in late summer or autumn because it will have a strong profile now. Even a hedge with a scalloped or castellated top, or fancy finials, can create an attractive array of shadows across the grass.

Sometimes the shadow patterns are happy accidents, but it is possible to anticipate where to plant for the best results. For example, when setting out a row of lollipop-headed standards or sharply pointed cones, make sure that the sun will be moving

Left Light, causing silhouettes, can bring about curious interactions between adjacent elements of topiary, green architecture and hedging. Here, a pyramid-shaped finial is mirrored by a shadowy replica.

Right The slanting light of autumn lengthens the shadows and produces some beautiful effects. This pathway is decorated with stripes caused by light shining between the stems of a stilt hedge.

around them in order to throw the shadows where they will be most effective. If you had a pathway that was lined with large, ball-headed standards of holly, holm oak or bay, at certain times of the day you would see a double row of circular shadows. Another interesting effect comes from light shining through ivy *treillage* panels, throwing grid-like patterns across adjacent lawns or paving. Aerial hedges on stilts (that is, bare trunks) also have great potential when they are positioned where the light passes through their legs, creating a series of soft parallel lines on the ground. Other structures, such as colonnades, can be equally effective. These special effects are just as successful enlivening a blank wall, provided that you think ahead.

Above The architectural quality of these holm oak cylinders, like giant stone pillars, is accentuated by the long shadows.

high definition

On bright days, the sculptural qualities of topiary really come to the fore as each facet catches the light in a different way, some being fully illuminated, and others in varying degrees of shadow. With the sun acting as a slow-moving directional spotlight, the sharp angles cut in green architecture and the geometry of shapes such as pyramids and spirals are greatly enhanced.

Topiary is often used to create a sense of depth and perspective in gardens, and the play of light and shadow on individual shapes, hedges and other structures is very much part of the illusion. At the Jardins d'Eyrignac, in the Dordogne,

France, the sense of drama experienced as you walk down the main *alleé*, lined with its complex, repeating pattern of green architecture, relies heavily on light and shade to produce sharp contrasts between adjacent pieces.

A more contemporary example of this effect is found in the private garden of Piet Oudolf, a Dutch landscape designer of international acclaim, where a striking feature is created by three hedges, set one in front of the other, each cut into

Below Complementing the architecture of the Château du Pin, this avenue of topiary is thrown into sharp relief by sunlight.

Above The vertical face of each element of this box parterre is in complete shadow, thus highlighting the texture and pattern of the horizontal surface.

Above As the sun moves round the garden during the day, the pattern of light and shade created by green architecture and topiary forms changes subtly.

undulating wave formations rather like pieces of scenery on a stage. One of the best gardens in Britain to study light and shadow is at Levens Hall, in Cumbria, England. Its large, quirky, eccentric, topiarized shapes are crowded into a relatively small area, producing a surreal "Alice in Wonderland" experience. On a bright day, the interaction of the pieces showing myriad shades of green makes the garden an artist's dream location.

Low hedge patterns, from simple compartmentalized designs to ornate *parterre de broderie* (where hedges are arranged in clipped, intricately intertwined shapes), also benefit from bright light which produces heavy contrasts between the horizontal and vertical surfaces, the latter appearing almost black. In knot gardens, particularly those clipped entirely from one type of plant, the interweaving, over-and-under design shifts magically as you walk past and the light catches the contours from different angles.

Another type of topiary, used to great effect at the Clipsham Yew Walk, in Rutland, where almost 150 large pieces form an imposing avenue, involves clipping various emblems and decorations in relief using the smooth, fine-grained surface of yew and box. Without strong side lighting, these monochrome designs can be very subtle. Topiary and green architecture are ideal subjects for artificial illumination, allowing us to enjoy a dramatic sculptural experience. Use mini-spot uplighters or mini floodlights to emphasize key features and contours, and do not be afraid of using coloured light for startlingly theatrical results.

ICE AND WATER

Whether it be in the form of still reflecting pools, cascades or sparkling fountains, green sculpture is enhanced immeasurably by water. And in its frozen state as ice or snow, water continues to work its magic, transforming topiary and formal hedging overnight.

A light scattering of snow will highlight every near-horizontal surface, turning quite simple shapes into exquisite sculptures, while complex forms like the spiral, cake stand or triple ball take on a fairy-tale quality. Clipped hedges with a stepped profile, buttresses or finials really come to life, and frost and snow also reveal every undulation of organic or free-form shapes and all the bumps, dips and knobs of billowing yew or box hedging. The texture of quite simple ground patterns, such as the basket-of-eggs design, is emphasized and each twist and turn of an interwoven knot garden is defined with startling clarity.

Heavy snow can make figurative topiary sculptures appear even more eccentric, the shapes balancing teetering dollops of white. But since the weight of snow can ruin fragile structures and cause breakages, brush the snow off vulnerable forms like the cake stand or cloud-pruned specimens at the first opportunity.

Frosted topiary is particularly worth viewing at close quarters. These solid structures are often covered in cobwebs, but they only reveal themselves on frosty or dewy mornings. After a heavy hoar frost the combination of lacy cobwebs and red fruits and berries can be enchanting.

Forward planning is recommended in order to make the most of a site and this section looks at the different ways in which you can incorporate water into both formal gardens of topiary and crisp green architecture, as well as more naturalistic settings.

Above left In early morning frost, the beauty of this armillary sphere and partnering box topiary is utterly captivating.

Above right This magnificent bird of prey, clipped freehand from shrubby honeysuckle (*Lonicera nitida*), is brought to life by frost.

Right Simple patterns, such as this arrangement of box cubes, are enhanced by frost settling on the horizontal surfaces.

cascades and fountains

The addition of a fountain can make all the difference to a garden of static green architecture, especially one which relies heavily on dark evergreen hedges and topiarized shapes.

The gardens of the Italian and French Renaissance are noted for their extravagant use of water, and include fountains and cascades which often required amazing feats of engineering. Few gardens could now accommodate fountain sculptures as opulent as those at Versailles, or jets as powerful as Joseph Paxton's Emperor Fountain at Chatsworth House, in Derbyshire, England. Fortunately, you can still find inspiration in the many formal gardens which include more modest water features, particularly those inspired by the Arts and Crafts movement.

The wonderful thing about some formal topiary gardens is the pervading sense of peace. They rely on just a few basic elements – stone or brick, topiary and hedging, lawns and, invariably, water. The power of the design comes from the clever use of a 2-D ground pattern and 3-D architecture, and the creation of clearly defined sight lines and vistas instead of colourful flowers and seasonal foliage. Fountains, water jets and cascades provide sufficient movement and sound to enliven these quiet green oases.

You can take advantage of the slightest change in level to incorporate a curtain-like fall of water in a rill or canal, but on a steeply sloping site there is plenty of opportunity for creating dramatic, stepped cascades. One trick is to highlight the changes in level with paired topiary pieces or stepped hedges placed either side of the water course. Small fountain jets look enchanting, springing up through complex patterns of a clipped box parterre and, where space is limited, try a wall fountain, decorated with potted box balls.

Above left A narrow rill feeds into a series of pools in this green room.

Above right Fountain jets add movement and sparkle to this space, emphasizing the airiness of the pleached trees in the background.

Left This modern interpretation of a parterre includes small fountain jets that spring from apertures in the box hedging. The glint of moving water brings the garden to life.

Right In this contemporary topiary garden, the designer incorporates polished stainless-steel water basins and fountain jets.

reflections

Water, in the form of geometrically shaped pools, canals and rills, has long been associated with formal gardens. Being fluid and reflective it makes the perfect foil for solid, man-made shapes like stonework, statuary, topiary and clipped hedging. Pools that mirror the sky and surrounding forms produce a subtly changing picture.

In many gardens, water is used to evoke an atmosphere of mystery and romance. Meandering through the formal park surrounding Château de Courances, near Fontainebleau, France, the long canals which radiate through the landscape seem magical in autumn with slanting light filtering down through the trees and mist hanging over the water's surface. And at the fairytale Château du Pin, in the Loire valley, where topiarized shapes like so many ladies dressed in crinolines gather round a pool, it is the water and its reflections which give the composition so much character.

Pools are often used to fill the central motif of a parterre, acting like a glinting jewel at the heart of the design, and in stone terraces or lawns planted with an assortment of topiary figures, the simplicity of a geometrically shaped reflective

Above In a formal topiary garden of quiet green shades, a still reflecting pool can introduce reflected light as well as provide a welcome contrast in texture.

Right At Château du Pin in the Loire valley, in France, the complex forms of matching yew topiaries are mirrored in the surface of a large formal pool.

surface creates a sense of space and serenity. Bordering a rectangular pool, canal or rill with a line of pencil-thin or dome-shaped forms is especially pleasing. On a much smaller scale, a tiny courtyard with a central, raised pool, perhaps encased by clipped box, can really make the garden feel larger because of the mirror-like quality of the water's surface.

New Wave topiarists experiment with all forms of the art, including organic and free-style clipping, and the undulating forms are ideal for edging the margins of naturalistic water features. The style has much in common with some traditional Japanese tea gardens where plants such as evergreen azaleas are clipped into rounded shapes like boulders, and cloud-pruned trees and shrubs arch elegantly over the still water.

Above The glassy surface of this pool is an essential component in this contemporary composition of yew columns.

GREEN
ARCHITECTURE

The many varied shapes and structures that
gardeners create by training and clipping plants
are described collectively as green architecture.
This section of the book comprises a catalogue
of classic elements, suggesting where each
might be used and what plants are best suited to
being trained into particular forms, as well as
practical hints and tips and several illustrated
step-by-step sequences.

Some elements, such as green walls and
colonnades, are so substantial that they would
cost a great deal more to construct from bricks
and mortar, dressed stone or *treillage* panels.
You might not want to wait for the plants to
grow but it is surprising how effective even an
embryonic framework can be, and how quickly
the feel of the garden changes once you
introduce a structure. Reputedly slow-growing
subjects, such as box and yew, begin to look
respectable by the third year, and decorative
topiary frames will create an instant impact.

Left This yew hedge has all the characteristics of an old brick or
stone wall with supporting buttresses of ornamental design and
regularly spaced "carved" finials.

Nowadays, the emphasis in the gardening world is very much on creating "instant gardens" and, as a result, some nurserymen and topiary importers offer living structures that are already part-trained in order to reduce the time you need to wait for the topiary to become established. Obviously, you will have to pay a premium for getting a head start but, if money is no object, then you could plant ready-grown and clipped box edging to outline a geometric parterre or substantial archways and arbours shaped from beech and hornbeam as well as pleached screens of lime. A wide range of "instant" hedging is also available which would create a sense of enclosure and maturity.

If you can afford to wait for your garden structures to grow from scratch, there are several advantages. Plants usually establish a better root system when grown in the ground from small potted specimens or bare-root material (lifted direct from the ground during the dormant period). If the garden is fairly exposed, you will have to support any ready-grown structures or provide windbreaks for quite some time – at least until the plants have produced a strong enough root system to anchor themselves into the ground and cope with the turbulence. Some kind of automatic irrigation system may also be necessary to make it easier to keep the plants alive during establishment.

Left The clipped box parterre gives this elegant courtyard a classical Italianate feel and the climber-clad wall, complete with porthole, provides another striking architectural feature. This is a garden made vibrant by the combined shapes and textures of the planting, as well as by the dynamic chequerboard paving.

Right A stilt hedge provides a strong architectural backdrop to this loosely formal garden of random stone paving, steps and a formal pool decorated with clipped topiary domes and cones and an abundance of herbaceous perennials.

Far left The off-kilter
entranceway in this hedge is
perfectly in keeping with the
carefree style of this old
country garden.

Left Clipped cubes at the four
corners of this little courtyard
garden help to define the
space and emphasize its
symmetry. The pretty blue chair
invites you to sit and pause for
thought and a spot
of reflection.

ARCHITECTURAL FEATURES

Living structures, such as archways, colonnades and walls, complete
with elaborate buttresses and finials, are a natural extension of the
architecture of the house. Such elements help to create the framework of
the garden as well as to furnish its rooms.

In today's small suburban and city gardens, the plot is often
dominated by the house and out of scale with its surroundings.
Trees provide structure and height, helping to redress the
balance, but they tend to take up a lot of room and may rob the
garden of light. On the other hand, geometric topiary figures,
such as clipped columns marking the entranceway or a stilt
hedge that defines the boundary, add shape and even a touch of
theatre, while still leaving plenty of scope for flowers.

Although many of the features in this section of the book
are most closely associated with period architecture, and are
an essential part of traditional formality, when simplified and
pared down to a basic shape or repeating pattern, they can work
just as effectively in contemporary settings.

The juxtaposition of the various structures and individual
elements also affects the look and feel of the garden. For
example, an asymmetrical layout and the placing of rectilinear
elements adjacent to contrasting free-form topiary, suggests
modernity – rather like avant-garde sculpture in an art gallery.
Meanwhile, symmetry with a high degree of embellishment
harks back to the Renaissance.

One of the most familiar and versatile pieces of green
architecture is the hedge and, although many people would not
classify hedging as a branch of topiary, an immaculately cut
formal divide shows great skill on behalf of the hedge trimmer.
Formal hedges are perfect for splitting a plot into intimate
rooms. You can keep things simple or take a more theatrical
approach, adding embellishments to your walls such as
niches and other detailing like flights of steps. Shaped doorways
and *clairvoyées* provide opportunities for creating exciting
views, while, in winter, a garden with architectural structure and
well-defined three-dimensional spaces, will continue to inspire.

Right A circular topiary "container" provides the perfect setting for
displaying this tiered cake stand.

hedges

Hedges can be viewed as garden barriers, divisions or enclosures, as well as living substitutes for walls and fences. Although labour intensive and not for instant effect, they have significant aesthetic advantages over brick and stone. Hedging is a softer alternative, usually coming in shades of green, and evergreen hedging in particular provides year-round continuity.

Hedges make a restful garden backdrop and those with a smooth, clipped, vertical surface provide a perfect foil for decorative flowers and foliage. When neatly maintained and

cut to a variety of eye-catching designs and profiles, green masonry can also dramatically enhance the structural lines of the garden.

At their simplest, formal hedges are cut with straight sides, a flat top and right-angle corners, all easily achievable with a long straight piece of wood, spirit level and plumb line. On a sloping site, you can step down the profile of the hedge in stages. A sloping face, known as a batter, with the base wider than the top, allows light to fall evenly, thereby preventing the bottom of

how to shape and renovate a hedge

Most deciduous hedging is planted in the dormant period and cut back by half immediately afterwards to promote dense branching. This process may be repeated the following year to encourage plants to knit together. With semi-evergreen privet and broad-leaved evergreens like laurel, however, cut back towards the end of summer. Begin clipping and shaping only once well established. Leave conifers to reach a little below the required height before removing the leading shoot.

To create buttresses, use several evenly spaced plants to cover the base and allow a section at the back to grow taller, while the rest are cut lower in steps or curved segments. Create finials by allowing shoots to grow up from the surface and clip them to shape using a wire former or train them freehand.

1 Formal hedging can be maintained with a hedge trimmer. Keep the blade parallel to the hedge surface to avoid taking out chunks of foliage. Take care with conifers since, with the exception of yew, most are reluctant to re-grow if you cut too far back into the brown interior.

2 Regenerate threadbare or overgrown hedging by cutting hard back into the old wood of plants such as yew, box, *Ligustrum ovalifolium* and beech. Cut one side of the hedge at a time, leaving a year's gap before tackling the other side of the hedge. Feed and water well.

Above Pleached screens and hedges raised on stilts trained from lime, box and hornbeam are perfect where space for planting is at a premium, as in this well-stocked garden.

Above The length of this hedge makes it an impressive architectural feature, containing, as it seems to do, the froth of flowers and other plants that are spilling over the edge.

the hedge from becoming threadbare. Poorly maintained hedges tend to develop the opposite profile and have a pronounced overhang which robs the base of light, causing bottom growth to be poor and patchy.

Imaginative designs might incorporate Rococo curves, castellations, buttresses and finials. You can make a wooden template to help snip out patterns, though most gardeners eventually end up doing this by eye, which is much quicker.

Electric or petrol hedge trimmers are a godsend for large runs, provided they are rested periodically to prevent the motor from burning out, and are properly maintained. When hand clipping with shears, alleviate the strain on your wrists by keeping one hand still, while working with the opposite arm, and then swap over. Also use a long bamboo cane to flick debris from the top of the hedge because, if left, it can lead to fungal infections in healthy branches. Mobile platforms and ladder stabilizers may be another worthwhile investment, especially for maintaining tall hedges with a greater degree of safety.

Right For this buttress, plant a block of yew and cut it roughly to create a series of steps. When the branches grow and fill out, then you can shape the bowed face.

blocks and steps

Square and rectangular blocks help to create an avant-garde look in the garden, perfect for minimalist urban spaces, but these topiarized shapes are some of the most difficult to create and maintain because even the smallest mistake shows up as a glaring error.

Rectangular blocks like chiselled masonry can be used to create a plinth effect around a statue or sculpture giving it more prominence. They can also be used like pieces of modern art in a sculpture park, set in isolation on a lawn, or to frame a formal pool.

In contemporary gardens, blocks can be embellished by having a simple shape, such as a wooden, metallic or stone pillar, rising out of the centre, while combining contrasting plants can also create an eye-catching effect. Consider, for example, using a square frame of golden yew with a block of dark green yew rising up from the centre. This is quite easy to achieve by planting a solid grid of dark yew surrounded by a row of less vigorous golden yews. On a smaller scale, try a block of box (*Buxus sempervirens*) with a frame of the cream-variegated *B. s.* 'Elegantissima'.

Blocks can also be refined to add extra interest. For example, a square shape might have a low dome rising from the centre or the top half of the block might be cut to resemble the facets of a gemstone or a simple pyramid.

Blocks don't have to be square or rectangular. You can create rhomboids, trapezoids and cheese wedges or design a chess set, sundial or starburst sculpture. You can even create a not-to-be-used flight of steps to link a lower garden with an upper terrace or deck. Fine-leaved box is ideal. Plant right across the area, spacing the young plants evenly. Grow them to the same height and then, using a series of taut lines, begin to cut steps into the block.

Left Here, a darker yew finial appears to sit on top of stepped box blocks, thus creating an interesting contrast of textures.

Left The square contouring on these blocks makes for a striking feature and shows how even very subtle shaping can be highly decorative.

Right Geometric topiary elements such as these need precision clipping to be successful. Notice how the shapes are lined up with the entranceway, taking the eye to the next garden room.

Below left Despite being in the grounds of an old French château, these giant, multifaceted blocks of yew stand like exhibits in a modern sculpture garden.

Below right These box steps are used as an architectural element, echoing the horizontal lines of the pergola and providing a contrast with the wild landscape beyond.

doorways and windows

Creating shaped apertures in a formal hedge – from circular windows to grand, classically styled arches – strengthens the illusion that the green "wall" is actually a substantial piece of architecture. Such elements also relieve the monotony of an otherwise featureless hedge by providing a focal point. The glimpse of another garden creates a sense of space within an enclosed area, while a hedge perforated by a series of vertical slits allows light through at the same time as maintaining a degree of privacy. Windows or *claivoyées*, as they once were known, engender an air of mystery by allowing tantalizing views of the landscape beyond. Carefully position apertures so that you frame an interesting view and not an eyesore!

A window can often be made just by cutting a hole through the hedge, perhaps capitalizing on a thin patch of branches. Simple shapes, for example circles, ovals and rectangles, are the easiest kind to maintain, and you can use a plywood template attached to a stake for initial training.

Above Conifers such as thuja and cupressus make dense, narrow forms. These two columns have been crossed over and tied together below the growing points, resulting in an architectural arch.

how to shape an arch

It is easy to add a theatrical touch by training an arched entrance. If you line up a series of arches, you could create a stunning formal *alleé*, leading the eye to a focal point.

Leave a wider than door-sized gap when planting the hedge, and continue to cut the frame as the hedge grows so that it has straight sides. When the hedge has grown beyond head height, allow the shooting side-branches to grow out towards each other. Train these branches into an arc, and encourage the shoots at the top to knit together to form a solid lintel. You may want to use a framework of canes to guide the branches across the gap but this will not be necessary with a fast-growing conifer hedge. Use a hedge trimmer to shape the top and vertical surfaces.

Above A gothic-arched doorway shapes the view at one end of a long topiary avenue that lines up perfectly with the château.

Above From darkness to light – an arched doorway frames the entrance to a Tuscan terrace.

When shaping screening plants with lax branches or a hedging plant like hawthorn which has an unruly habit, fix branches to an arched metal frame and continue to clip to shape. Frames can also help to define more architectural shapes such as the gothic arch.

Above A carefully planned aperture in a boundary hedge offers views of the wild landscape beyond.

niches and alcoves

In a classically inspired formal garden, the creation of niches and alcoves provides elegant spaces where statuary, obelisks, flower-filled vases, seats and other objects may be highlighted.

A shallow niche can usually be clipped out of a mature hedge provided the growth is quite dense and uniform. Take care with quick-growing conifers such as × *Cupressocyparis leylandii* which may not regenerate well if you cut back to the brown inner branches. Niches are particularly interesting when the face of the hedge has a batter or slope to contrast with its perpendicular shape. Clip the shape to the required height and width to comfortably accommodate the object in question.

A rectangular niche is the easiest shape to attempt, for which you'll only need a plumb line, straight edge and spirit level. Otherwise make a template or use a can of water-based spray paint to mark the shape on the hedge. Niches in a period setting look more authentic with an elegantly curved top – perfect for featuring ball-headed standards in terracotta pots or Versailles planters. For a really eye-catching feature, you could add

Below In this garden inspired by the Arts and Crafts movement, a simple stone seat, perfect for moments of quiet reflection, is hidden from view by an arbour of clipped yew.

evergreen pillars or columns at the side. Niches can also be left empty; one by itself looks like a mistake, but a repeating pattern creates textural variation in a long, flat-faced hedge of beech or yew, for example. These shapes come to life when the sun moves round and creates dark shadow patterns. Large, semi-circular alcoves, known as *exedrae*, should be planned at hedge-planting time.

When making a shelter for a bench seat, instead of carving your way deep into a hedge, you could simply grow out the sides and top to form an arbour. A rustic-style arbour cut from a hedge of holly, hawthorn or privet is ideal in a country or cottage garden. To speed up the process, you can also plant to the front of the hedge, forming the left- and right-hand verticals and training the branches up to form the arched roof.

Above This dramatic hornbeam hedge resembles a colonnade with its square-profile pillars and deep recesses.

Above Narrow grooves clipped into this high hornbeam hedge provide a pleasing visual rhythm. The strong sunlight, which produces dark shadows, accentuates the contrast.

Right Deep curving *exedrae* such as this are planned from the beginning of the garden's design. Here, the curved yew bay makes an ideal setting for a piece of sculpture.

tunnels and yew houses

Creating contrasting areas of sun and shadow within the garden adds to the sense of drama. Leafy tunnels can be particularly effective with the subdued green light and feeling of enclosure engendering a sense of magic and mystery. Meandering tunnels, or those with a gentle curve, create even more suspense because you are unable to see the end as you peer into the darkness at the entrance.

Yew tunnels develop an incredible structure, both inside and out, and those that are associated with historic houses are often thought to be much older than they really are. The longest-living creations with gnarled, twisted, arching trunks might look

1,000 years old but, once a dendrologist is brought in to run some tests, the figure is usually found to be closer to 200–300 years.

An airy alternative to the yew tunnel is the *berceau*, which in formal gardening usually applies to a shady, trellis-covered pergola walkway covered in closely trained plants with viewing apertures or windows. Hornbeam is the traditional choice, but you could also use a climber, for example a vigorous ivy such as *Hedera helix* 'Green Ripple'.

Colonnades are highly theatrical features for the garden, having overtones of classical architecture and, in fact, the arches make the perfect setting for pieces of Greco-Roman statuary, and stone or terracotta urns and vases. With a bit of imagination you could create the feel of a Tuscan villa garden in the heart of surburbia. Many amateur gardeners might think the colonnade far too challenging, but it is simply a series of connected archways. Plant your hedge, leaving gaps at regular intervals, and train the arches. Stilt hedges, pleached screens and colonnades are sufficiently light and airy to frame a pathway and so can be incorporated into quite small gardens where light is often at a premium.

Another quirky topiary feature is the yew house, which may be a completely enclosed clipped dome with an entrance that provides access to the cool, dark interior – a secret retreat for children and adults alike. Alternatively, a crescent of yews can be trained to form a seamless enclosure and canopy over a garden seat. Equally rustic is the parasol design in which a central trunk, with a circular seat around the base, is topped by a giant umbrella or mushroom-like shape.

Left This quaint yew house, cut with a mushroom-shaped head, is supported by four posts which also help to give a more structured form to the arbour.

Right The roof of this arched walkway in lime is formed by training the branches over a frame.

stilt hedging and pleaching

In the ancient art of pleaching, the soft pliable stems of certain trees are trained horizontally along taut wires run between vertical posts. The base of the slender screen is usually positioned above head height so that you can walk up an avenue of bare tree trunks.

The advantage of pleaching is that a substantial structural element can be introduced into a relatively small space. And, because the branches are quite widely spaced and only grown in one plane, they create minimal shade while, in winter, after leaf fall, the overall structure is still very effective. In addition, the ground below a pleached screen can be cultivated, and the bare legs can be used to frame views into the garden beyond.

Pleached screens are most commonly used to create boundaries and internal divides, to enclose sections or terraces without robbing them of light, and to line paths or create formal avenues. Various species and cultivars of lime (*Tilia*) are most commonly used, but you can also try climbers such as grape vine (*Vitis vinifera*), *Laburnum* x *watereri* 'Vossii', wisteria and

Below Pleached screens can be set parallel to one another to form a shady walkway with open sides allowing views of the garden.

Below The trunks of a stilt hedge or pleached screen are reminiscent of a stone colonnade.

rose, training the "rods" or main framework of stems horizontally, which encourages flowering and fruiting. You can buy ready-trained plants from specialists which have a framework of branches attached to horizontal bamboo canes. When starting from scratch, some leafy side shoots are left on the main stems to help them thicken and strengthen. To create a cool walkway of dappled shade, train a pleached screen roof by extending the framework of wires at right angles.

The stilt hedge is a variation on this theme, and uses plants like hornbeam which have a dense branching habit. The raised hedge has a formal profile and, once the basic training is finished, the supports are removed and the growth is clipped in the normal way. Unlike hedges that grow up from ground level and form a solid barrier, stilt hedges allow cold air to percolate through, thereby avoiding the creation of a frost pocket.

Above You can create a covered walkway if you extend the wire training framework of a pleached lime screen.

Below The bowed branches of this espalier apple are laden with fruit.

PATTERNED PLANTING

A number of different kinds of topiary are used to decorate the garden floor and the designs can be admired either at close quarters or from a higher vantage point. Designs can occupy a large area, such as hedge mazes, but typically patterns can be broken down for smaller gardens.

The spaces left between the low clipped hedges of the knot garden, certain types of parterre as well as the potager, are often planted to further enhance the decorative effect. Seasonal bedding, including spring bulbs and biennials, as well as annuals and tender perennials that bloom through summer into autumn with a minimum of maintenance, are popular choices.

Colours that show up well against dark green foliage are favoured for creating dramatic schemes that must stand out clearly over a large area, but in smaller gardens with a more intimate atmosphere, muted pastels are often preferred. Single varieties, as opposed to mixtures, are used to maintain the pattern's high definition and plants for bold summer colour might include violet *Verbena × hybrida*, scarlet, fibrous-rooted begonias or cerise-pink Busy Lizzies (F1 hybrid *Impatiens*).

In potagers, ornamental varieties of herbs and vegetables are planted in bold blocks, resulting in an attractive as well as potentially productive growing area. Foliage plants might include ornamental kale; ruby chard; decorative lettuce varieties and variegated sage or thyme. Care must be taken in the choice of these "filler" plants, however, because they must not overwhelm the topiary. This could cause the foliage to die back and would mar the effect of the often complex patterns.

More permanent infill plantings are possible to cut down on maintenance. For example, within a simple knot made from dwarf box, you could use silvery plants or white-variegated evergreens for contrast, such as cotton lavender (*Santolina chamaecyparissus* 'Lemon Queen'); dwarf lavenders such as 'Munstead' or 'Hidcote'; certain small-leaved hebes; or *Euonymus fortunei* 'Emerald Gaiety'. These would only need clipping once a year and could be grown to create a flat-topped block of colour or to create a "basket-of-eggs" texture.

Right Against box, pink- and red-coloured flowers, as well as white and yellow, stand out vividly.

knots and parterres

The Elizabethans were fascinated by complex, intertwining patterns including knots, puzzles and artfully combined initials. They can be found in period buildings in the form of carved wood and plasterwork panels, as well as in costume detail such as embroidered fabrics and ruffs. In the garden, there was an opportunity to design living knots using many familiar herb garden plants, including lavender, cotton lavender (*Santolina*), wall germander (*Teucrium chamaedrys*), hyssop, shrubby thyme, marjoram, pennyroyal (*Mentha pulegium*) and box, all clipped to form low hedges.

Symmetrical designs, such as an overlaying of circles and squares, are relatively easy to create and, today, the choice of plants is much wider. As well as variegated box cultivars you can use forms of Japanese holly, such as *Ilex crenata* 'Golden Gem', varieties of *Euonymus fortunei* (especially 'Emerald Gaiety' and 'Emerald 'n' Gold'), and the purple-leaved dwarf barberry (*Berberis thunbergii* f. *atropurpurea* 'Atropurpurea Nana').

When clipped with precision, the differently coloured plants appear to weave in and out, under and over. This is pure illusion, of course, a result of making parts of the latticework slightly higher where they cross over. This style works particularly well when the hedges are shaped to give a rounded profile. Although the spaces between the hedges are sometimes filled with plants, the Elizabethan method of using coloured earth shows the pattern most clearly, and is easier to maintain. There is now a wide choice of aggregates, including fine gravel and coloured stone chippings.

Above A bold knot, consisting of threads of two contrasting box cultivars, is clipped in an accentuated fashion to suggest an over-and-under interweaving.

Right The complex, curling patterns of *parterre de broderie* are best defined with a simple background of pale gravel or stone chippings.

Above You do not need a large formal garden in order to accommodate a parterre. Simple designs of low hedging can work well in small spaces.

Above Although they tend to have a less well-defined structure, knots that are planted with herbs such as bushy thymes work well in a sunny spot.

Unlike the knot garden, the parterre consists of shapes, outlines or compartments that are separate. Several distinct styles of parterre developed over time, some rigidly geometric, others very flamboyant. The *parterre de broderie* consisted of elegant motifs that were inspired by flowers, leaves and curling tendrils, mostly fashioned from clipped dwarf box. The infilling or highlighting of parterres was usually done with coloured earth, crushed stone or turf, the latter painstakingly cut by hand.

Some techniques were highly labour intensive, including the arabesque forms of cutwork-in-the-English-manner, with shapes being carved out of lawn and infilled with coloured aggregate. After the grand parterres inspired by the French Renaissance were stripped away in favour of a more naturalistic landscaping style, the parterre did not make a significant comeback until the Victorian era when, once again, highly ornate patterns on a dramatic scale became very popular. The shapes were filled with brilliantly coloured bedding plants and sub-tropical foliage. Whatever pattern or technique appeals to you, bear in mind that the greater the complexity of the design, the more important it is that the plants are maintained in excellent health and are regularly clipped and tidied.

Above Water features such as pools and fountains counter the static nature of a parterre.

mazes

The history of the maze can be traced back into antiquity but, as with topiary, there have been periods of great popularity and also of declining interest. The Italian Renaissance was one of the highpoints when garden architects loved incorporating all kinds of extra ingredients, such as trick fountains, to soak the unwary. As the Renaissance movement spread across Europe, more wealthy garden owners, especially members of the aristocracy, included mazes in their formal grounds and no doubt discovered the advantages of high hedges – secluded areas for secret meetings or romantic liaisons. The use of classical statuary, including gods and mythical creatures, added to the fantasy setting. Right at the heart of the maze the reward was usually a small secret garden, like a jewel that awaited discovery.

The Victorians were also fond of mazes and, along with parterres, they began to feature in public parks for the enjoyment of all and not just the wealthy.

Although labyrinths, with their pagan and later Christian symbolism, were certainly a precursor of the maze the latter is essentially a puzzle to be solved by the players, the aim of the exercise usually being to reach the centre and have fun losing your way *en route*. In today's gardens there are a great variety of mazes, including pavement mazes and even those made from colourful mosaics, but hedging mazes are the only kind that we

are concerned with here. There are countless layouts to choose from, and you'll find several specialist books on the subject as well as some excellent internet sites featuring classical patterns and more avant-garde designs. A child's puzzle book can also be a rich source of ideas.

Mazes can be planted as they were in Tudor and Elizabethan times using knee-high hedges of lavender, cotton lavender or slow-growing box, all of which are great for children. But for the more effective, taller, dense evergreen kind, go for yew, holly or laurel or a quick-growing hedging conifer.

Above Mazes can take almost any form in order to suit the size and shape of the land available.

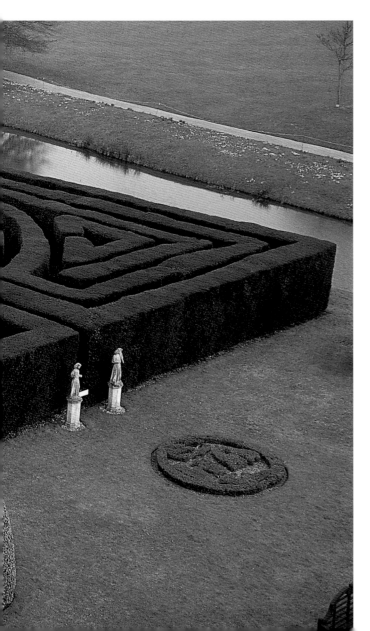

Left Although you can see the solution to the puzzle from above, this maze at Hever castle, in Kent, England, presents a real challenge.

labyrinths

Steeped in myth and legend, the exact origins and meanings of ancient labyrinths, often designed with intricate patterns, are now lost. Turf labyrinths are thought to have been designed for contemplation and as a place to meditate on one's faith while walking the pathways. Similar designs appear in Bronze Age stone carvings called petroglyphs. As well as turf labyrinths there are also smooth pavement designs and ones marked out with rocks. Many, but not all, are situated close to religious centres, within or next to churches, cathedrals or monasteries.

Turf labyrinths were once widely found across most of Europe, but there are now only a handful in existence, largely confined to England and Germany where they have long been associated with local traditions and festivities. Often a sacred tree was set at the centre of the labyrinth. Unlike traditional mazes that are frequently rectilinear in design, the turf labyrinth is usually constructed with curving lines and patterns reminiscent of Celtic or prehistoric symbols. A popular form is the rounded Chartres design which has been traced back to the

13th century. This is a fascinating labyrinth because as hard as you try to walk to the centre, the pathway frequently forces you back out to the rim. The form is perfectly suited to the New Age garden, which might include organic shapes and sacred symbols, but equally, the turf labyrinth can be used to create an intriguing motif in the lawn, especially one that can be viewed from above. The element of fun is a draw for children who love darting along the narrow twisting, turning pathways to reach the middle.

In turf labyrinths, the sunken paths are either left as bare, compacted soil or are covered with stone chippings or brick. The grass ridges reach to just above ankle height with a rounded profile. It goes without saying that unless regularly walked and maintained with a strimmer, the labyrinth will soon disappear. Traditional designs can be copied from specialist books and internet sites, and can be embellished, extended or reduced to fit the available space.

Below left This turf labyrinth of raised organic form blends seamlessly into the landscape of water and rolling hills beyond – the perfect setting for peaceful reflection.

Below right Although this is technically a maze puzzle, the form is cut into the turf like a labyrinth. The setting is rendered still more atmospheric by the early morning light.

Far left In combination and set against the natural form of a blue cedar, these topiary figures act like pieces of modern sculpture.

Left Being one of the more gentle geometric forms, domes suit relaxed, country-garden settings.

GEOMETRIC SHAPES

Ideal for adding a note of formality to the garden, spheres and domes, pyramids and cones, and cylinders and turrets are just a few of the mathematically precise forms that can be incorporated into the design as pieces of clipped topiary.

Though usually trained as stand-alone figures, different geometric shapes can also be combined in the form of tiered standards. Grow them surmounted on clipped blocks or columns for emphasis or as finials on top of formal hedging. They can be part of a highly structured landscape such as a contemporary minimalist garden or one based on classical principles. Alternatively, they provide dramatic contrast set against a relatively naturalistic backdrop. The more gentle, rounded forms, such as the snail-shell helix, and large domes can also work well in a semi-formal garden, adding just the right amount of structure, while being in keeping with the carefree atmosphere.

Such strong, solid shapes, when well proportioned and neatly clipped, act rather like chiselled stone masonry. Because of this, individual shapes are often used to strengthen the ground plan at key points and engender a feeling of ordered calm. Used in rows and patterns, geometric topiary forms set up visual rhythms in the garden. In matching pairs, the shapes add

weight and importance to entranceways, and, used singly, bold shapes can act as full stops or exclamation marks at the end of a vista or sight line, just like pieces of sculpture.

Perfection is something to be striven for when training this type of topiary – blocks, pyramids and the like being so far removed from anything in nature. There's no room for sloppy shaping, especially when creating a highly architectural set piece. An array of different elements could be combined in the surrounds of a modern building to create a texturally rich green garden that relies on perspective and the interaction of different forms instead of flower colours. You could make an asymmetric arrangement of rectangular reflecting pools, pergolas, formal hedges and topiary pieces and contrast these with the untrained forms of trees or banks of billowing organic topiary.

Right The rigidity of these clipped pyramids is beautifully offset by the diaphanous pink planting of cosmos.

pillars and cake stands

Classic topiary obelisks mirror those made from carved stone, having a square cross-section that tapers to a pyramid-shaped top. DIY frames made from dark green stained wood infilled with chicken wire make for easy training and the foliage eventually grows through the mesh to cover it completely. Clip the top into a pyramid or the equally popular ball shape. With such a strong profile, these structures are ideal for creating focal points in a formal setting, such as at the end of a central path or

pergola walkway. Decorative *treillage* frames make a bold impression long before the plant inside has started to fill the centre. You can highlight the contrast between the trelliswork and the interior of dark, evergreen foliage by staining or painting the wood in a paler shade. Although it is tempting to use several plants to fill out the base of a large frame quickly, this is a short-term solution that can lead to problems when the plants at the centre become starved of light. It is far better to use one well-grown plant with a single leading shoot. Yew is ideal, having such a fine-grained finish, but you can also use holly, *Phillyrea*, or, for warmer climes, Japanese yew (*Podocarpos macrophyllus*). And for especially quick results, try growing a dark green English ivy over the surface of a lightweight metal frame.

One pillar-like plant that requires very little training is the fastigiate or Irish yew (*Taxus baccata* 'Fastigiata') which also has some very attractive golden forms. To keep the column slim and to prevent the branches splaying out, maintain a single leader and cut back any additional leaders that appear around the sides.

Other topiary creations have a more pronounced modular structure and are reminiscent of totem poles since sections may have contrasting designs. Such structures are usually cut freehand. One of the most simple yet eye-catching looks rather like a tiered cake stand. There are several variations on this theme. If you intend the segments to be close together the structure can often be clipped from an existing column or cone shape provided it has a central stem. Some types of holly, such as *Ilex aquifolium*, naturally produce branches in tiers, which can be clipped to give greater definition.

Left These large, domed topiaries are topped with rounded finials which are relatively easy to shape freehand.

Right Like tapering chimneystacks, these topiaries make a change from traditional obelisks or tall narrow pyramids.

Above The work of an experienced topiary technician, these immaculate cake stands are clipped with mathematical precision.

Above To achieve this shape, a single leader has been trained up from the centre of a block of yew and shaped into a series of tiers.

Above Simple tiered forms with relatively thick sections could be shaped from a mature plant with a central leader.

spheres and domes

The most popular topiary figures are those with a simple, rounded profile. Not only are they invaluable for establishing a rhythm, framing entrances and defining the ground plan of a formal garden, but they can also be used to add structure and to inject pleasing shapes and textures into a mixed border.

Domes are particularly easy to train, and can be created using a wide range of plants. Some topiarists favour the dome over the sphere because the shape receives even light and therefore does not go bald at the base. Evergreen contenders include the olive-green *Hebe rakaiensis* and box cultivars such as *Buxus microphylla* 'Green Pillow' and *B. sinica* var. *insularis* 'Tide Hill', which have a natural, bun-shaped habit and require very little clipping. Yew and holly are favourites for large domes, but you can also try the quick-growing Portugal laurel (*Prunus lusitanica*) or *Viburnum tinus*. Silver-leaved *Brachyglottis* Dunedin Group 'Sunshine', plain or variegated *Euonymus japonicus* cultivars, bushy camellias and the tender, glossy-leaved *Pittosporum tobira* are good alternatives. For a finer

Above Box balls in terracotta pots are classic topiary icons. A similar, more easily managed shape is the dome, which is less likely to go thin at the base.

Left Evergreen balls and spheres work well in the mixed border, adding pleasing shape and structure, especially in winter, but without being too formal.

texture, in addition to yew, box, Japanese holly (*Ilex crenata*) and *Ligustrum delavayanum*, there are shrubby honeysuckle (*Lonicera nitida*), small-leaved, evergreen cotoneasters and scented *Osmanthus* x *burkwoodii*. For petite domes, compact lavenders, *Euonymus fortunei* cultivars, myrtle, small-leaved hebes and *Santolina chamaecyparissus* are worth trying.

Box forms like the compact-growing *Buxus microphylla* 'Faulkner' are ideal for producing a fine-textured ball or dome and, in a modern setting, try planting them in tall galvanized pots.

Below A change from green, these blue *Chamaecyparis* domes mark out the boundary of a little, Italian-style pool garden.

Above Combining shapes can create more prominent topiary features. Here, a collar has been added to a sphere.

pyramids and cones

One of the classic geometric shapes, the cone is simple to produce and extremely versatile. The shape can vary, ranging from slender, sharply pointed types to broad, spreading, blunt-ended creations. The former suit modern architectural gardens, and look striking when repeated and placed equidistantly either in a row or a chequerboard layout. The latter can be used individually or in pairs in a relaxed country-garden setting. Cones work well in containers, and are also frequently used to highlight key points in the garden design.

To shape a cone, begin with a plant that has a single main shoot or leader in the centre, and a generally upright habit. That way the plant will remain balanced during training, and won't break apart or become lopsided. Stand over the plant and step back at regular intervals, clipping the required shape. When trimming and shaping quite radically, it sometimes pays to work

Above Slender pyramids clipped from yew create an avenue of structure that comes into its own in winter.

in stages, delaying subsequent clippings to allow the plant time to recover and produce a fresh flush of dense, even foliage. If you are not confident about shaping by eye, either buy a cone-shaped frame to drop over the existing plant and cut off any protruding growth, or create a home-made frame consisting of a wigwam of bamboo canes. The base of each cane is pushed into the earth, and the frame can be removed when the basic shape has been established.

Egyptian-style pyramids make an impressive sight, but the proportions and angles need to be spot on. Start with a drawing or model, and scale up the dimensions so that you have precise figures to follow when constructing the frame. Pyramids made from equilateral triangles will be quite low and squat, but you can also create narrow forms with a sharply pointed top, ideal for creating avenues and vistas. Yew is an excellent choice, but you could also use holly, holm oak or beech, the latter making an interesting colour contrast against surrounding evergreens during the winter months.

Above right Teamed with a variegated hosta in a terracotta pot, a pair of potted cones, clipped from cream-variegated *Buxus sempervirens* 'Elegantissima', add an elegant accent to this doorway.

Left In this modern plot, a series of broad yew pyramids adds tremendously to the style and character of the garden, helping to link in with the historic surroundings.

Right The line of dark yew pyramids in this immaculately kept garden looks stunning against a backdrop of autumn colour, and helps to establish a sight line, leading the eye to the landscape beyond.

cylinders and turrets

Large, cylindrical pieces of topiary were historically used to create imposing avenues, perhaps leading to a point in the distant landscape. But the lone cylinder is a fascinating, eye-catching shape and can become a dramatic focus when dropped into a mixed border full of sculptural foliage plants, or when paired with other geometric forms, such as a pyramid or dome, in a contemporary design.

In fact, an existing plant can sometimes be given a new lease of life by superimposing the well-defined outline of a cylinder on its uneven form. Likely candidates for this treatment include broad conical or columnar conifers, for example the coloured-leaf forms of thuja and chamaecyparis, holly and bay trees. Yew and the holm oak (*Quercus ilex*) – a holly look-alike – are the traditional favourites for large cylinders, but you could also use boxwood, holly or privet (*Ligustrum ovalifolium*). In temperate regions this vigorous hedging privet remains virtually evergreen during mild winters.

The cylinder is cut with a flat top. Take care to use a cane to flick off any debris after clipping to prevent the spread of rot. To be absolutely accurate when cutting, check the sides using a plumb line.

A turret is a good variation, and can have straight or slightly tapering sides with a shaped top – imagine a giant pepper pot with a domed or cone-shaped lid. Turrets act like stone fortifications in the garden, set within or at the end of a formal hedge, or used in pairs like sentry boxes to frame an entrance.

Far left In large gardens, you can afford to add substantial structures. Architectural elements, such as this grand avenue of holm oak cylinders, which resemble massive stone pillars, create a powerful sense of drama.

Left For this type of formal topiary feature to work, the cylinders need to have the appearance of carved stonework. They look most convincing just after clipping.

Below left Add variety to a boundary feature or avenue by using two different geometric shapes and cultivars. Here, golden yew domes alternate with dark green yew cylinders.

Below right Fastigiate yews have a habit of sprawling outwards at the top unless they are rigidly pruned from the outset. Here, this tendency has been capitalized on in order to create unusual fluted shapes.

spirals and helter-skelters

Spirals have sufficient presence to be used individually, but they also work well as matching pairs, perhaps flanking a front door or another entrance within the garden, and they can even be planted in small groups to great effect. Spirals differ in form quite dramatically, from full-bodied figures with voluptuous curves to those with slender coils which look like a leafy garland twisted around a bare pole.

The slender-coiled kind can be tricky because they take longer to train than the full-bodied kind, which can be clipped almost instantly, and demand more skill from the topiarist. You will often see them grown from relatively quick-growing conifers such as juniper, thuja and chamaecyparis. They also tend to be quite expensive to buy. However, some of these swirling forms are not as difficult to create as you might think.

Above Spiral topiary can be created in different sizes, which means it can be incorporated in a variety of gardens, including small courtyard spaces or, as here, on a terrace.

Above Spirals are dynamic elements that suggest movement. Though often used in pairs to flank a doorway, grouping spirals randomly can create a more contemporary look.

Box is ideal for clipping small to medium-sized spirals in containers, but yew is better for producing large specimens grown in the ground.

When training a spiral, you can put your own individual stamp onto the design because there are several variables. At one extreme there is the squat snail shell which has very broad coils and only a shallow-cut groove. This means that the coils lie on top of each other with no gaps. If you can imagine attaching a string to the tip and pulling upwards to separate the coils slightly, then you have the next variant whereby the coils are set at a more pronounced angle. This angle, coupled with the width of the coils, suggests varying

Above The lazy coils of a bright green conifer helter-skelter make a wonderful visual contrast with the dark yew blocks and hedges of this highly architectural garden.

degrees of motion, from lazy turns to dynamic twists. Sometimes a spiral groove is clipped into a column instead of a cone, and you can also create near-horizontal coils clipped to resemble a gentle helter-skelter.

Whatever shape you decide on, do not worry if your spiral is not mathematically perfect or if an existing topiary begins to drift from the original design, with a pronounced lean or unravelling top. Topiary often ends up being quirky or eccentric.

Unlike symmetrical shapes that are static in nature, spirals are brimming with energy and movement. One important point to remember is that you must plan for the eventual size required. You cannot start with a small spiral and grow on a larger, identical version – you would need to add to the number of coils or merge existing coils and reshape.

how to clip a spiral

1

2

3

1 Start with a cone that has been clipped several times to create dense growth. If you intend to make deep cuts, the specimen should have a single leader from which all the side branches radiate. Tie a piece of string or raffia to the top of the plant and wind it around in a spiral, angling the string along the diagonal to make a tapering coil. Match the string to natural gaps in the foliage. The number of turns will depend on the height of the plant – typically three or five.

SUITABLE PLANTS

Upright growing species and cultivars with fine foliage such as:

Buxus sempervirens (box)

Chamaecyparis

Juniperus (juniper)

Laurus (bay laurel, sweet bay)

Taxus baccata (yew)

Thuja

2 Use a pair of secateurs (pruners), small hand shears or sheep shears to cut the initial groove using the string as a guide. Go gently at first, working from the top down and trying to keep the bands as even as possible. Work your way to the centre, cutting out any larger branches with the secateurs.

3 Continue to clip, deepening the groove and creating a coil with a rounded profile. Finally, stand the plant in a sheltered environment, providing optimum growing conditions that will help the plant recover and fill out quite quickly. Clip in spring and late summer to maintain the shape.

Right This box spiral, clipped to expose the central stem, appears to be made from a green garland coiled around a wooden post.

standards

With a shape such as a simple globe, dome, cone or stylized bird, held at the top of a slender stem, the topiary standard is certainly elegant. Whatever the design, topiary standards will add a touch of style to your garden. Consider them as potted sculptures for the terrace; rising up above a sea of planting in the border or paired with an identical twin to frame a gateway. Many gardeners have experience of making standards using quick-growing tender perennials such as fuchsias and marguerite daisies (*Argyranthemum*) and the same techniques are used for creating standards of box, bay, holly and so on.

Potted box standards are ideal for small, suburban gardens because the plants are quite dainty and the thickness and length of the stem stays in proportion to the size of the head. Problems may arise with other plants, such as the small-leaved privet (*Ligustrum delavayanum*), now a popular substitute for box which is only really suitable for tall standards with a relatively large head because the stem is naturally quite stout.

Ideally, start with a rooted cutting that has not yet been "pinched out". You might find suitable seedlings in the garden, such as *Viburnum tinus* or holly (*Ilex aquifolium*). Alternatively, buy young plants, such as variegated holly or bay , that have a single unbranched leader tied to a cane. Remove side shoots that form, but for the moment leave any foliage on the stem because this helps strengthen the leg. Once the leader has been trained to a little below the finished height, pinch out the top bud to encourage a head of new shoots to form. Instant standards can also be shaped from a bushy specimen provided you can see that there is a central, reasonably straight stem. The stem of standards trained from scratch can be formed into a corkscrew by winding them around a central pole while still soft and pliable. This is later removed. Climbers, such as *Plumbago auriculata* and honeysuckle (*Lonicera periclymenum*), can also be turned into standards by plaiting several stems around a permanent cane support and then shaping the head.

Right The spiral coils of a *Cryptomeria* cultivar give this conifer standard the appearance of a mop head.

Far right This bay standard's coiled leg was formed by winding the young, developing stem around a support pillar.

Above Two delicate birds clipped from box have been given an even more elegant air by virtue of being mounted on a slender leg or stem.

Far left Here, a ball-headed standard of *Buxus sempervirens* 'Elegantissima' rises above carpeting plants, adding light and definition.

Left The stem of this tall standard is especially smooth and straight, sitting neatly at right angles to the beautifully clipped hedge.

Buy a mature, dense, bushy plant with a clear upright stem at the centre. This plant must be the correct height for the final standard as it will fill out rather than grow taller. The treatment may seem rather drastic, but the head soon starts to develop ready for further shaping.

how to train a standard

1

2

3

4

SUITABLE PLANTS

Buxus sempervirens (box)

Cupressus (cypress)

Laurus (bay laurel, sweet bay)

Lonicera nitida (shrubby honeysuckle)

Ilex aquifolium (common holly)

Osmanthus (false or sweet holly)

Rosmarinus officinalis (rosemary)

1 Cut off all the branches emerging from the base to leave one single upright stem with side shoots along its length. Remove most of the side shoots up to the base of the proposed head, but retain a few individual feathery leaf shoots to help the main trunk to grow in strength.

2 Begin to shape the head by shortening the side shoots to form a rough ball. Cut out the shoot tip of the leading growth to encourage side shoots to form. Pinch out other shoot tip buds with thumb and forefinger.

3 Tie the stem to a vertical cane that reaches to the the base of the ball of shoots. Continue shaping the head to the desired shape as it grows. Give the plant some slow release fertilizer to encourage growth and water well. Stand in a sheltered spot away from direct sunlight and wind.

4 When clipping the final shape, flip the shears over so that the blades follow the curve of the ball. Continue to pinch off any leaves or shoots that appear on the stem or leg of the standard.

Above The finished topiary standard against a beech hedge.

The beauty of ivy topiary is that you can create the impression of classical topiary relatively quickly. Ivy-covered frames work well in pots and are ideal for the smaller garden. Simple frames, such as a 2-D star or heart, can be made from heavy-gauge galvanized wire.

how to make framed ivy topiary

1

2

3

4

NOTE
When creating a spiral, several stems are wound around a coil and trained together until they reach the top. For a standard, the stems are twisted together up the main stem and then trained out to cover the head. Finally, the leaves on the leg are pinched off.

1 Select plain green ivy plants, preferably those with long stems in order to achieve quick results. Pick a variety of ivy that has short "joints" or internodes (that is, the space between the buds) because this will produce compact growth with a good coverage of foliage, and will not be so vigorous that it swamps the frame. Push the frame into position and then plant the ivies around the rim of the pot so that the stems are next to the base of the frame. The same technique applies to any framed ivy topiary shape.

2 Wind the stems of the ivy plants around the upright struts. There is usually no need to tie them in position since the leaf bases act like grappling hooks. Try to create an even coverage of foliage.

3 As the plants grow, continue to spread out the new shoots until all of the frame is covered.

4 Thereafter, trim off any excess foliage in order to maintain the spiral shape. Feed regularly with liquid fertilizer.

Above The finished ivy spiral is neatly trained and will soon fill out.

LIVING SCULPTURE

Topiary is an incredibly malleable art form and some of the shapes and methods of training and clipping create sculptural elements that can delight or amaze. Sometimes, as with more organic, free-flowing topiary, the results are entirely abstract. But in other circumstances, such as Eastern cloud pruning, when representations of ancient, windblown trees are created, the subjects are definable. Animals are a favourite for green sculpture – either as moss-filled and framed topiaries or trained by eye. In formal gardens, as well as traditional peacocks and heraldic lions, you might see shrubs clipped in the form of classical vases or urns.

Meanwhile, in more avant-garde settings there are simply no limits. Perhaps you'd like to surprise passers-by with a giraffe or crocodile on your front lawn? And, if you aren't too confident about converting your hedge or favourite shrub into a piece of art, you can usually find a frame to guide you.

Left The combination of different geometric shapes, all formed from yew, creates a striking and dynamic architectural feature in this garden. They resemble stonework in their neat precision.

Choosing the right setting for your topiary work is an important part of the process. Sometimes the location dictates the subject matter for your latest artistic project. A relaxed cottage or informal country garden could be decorated with farmyard animals or native wildlife – birds, rabbits and so on. Next to a pool, you could have wading birds or some aquatic creature; alongside a drive, perhaps a vintage racing car. Finials may be geometric in design or sheer flights of fancy. Personal preferences and moods will also have an important influence.

Right A layer of ivy has been encouraged to grow over a series of posts, softening this boundary and at the same time creating a kind of abstract living sculpture, perfectly in keeping with the site.

Below Putting figures together like this pair of chlorophyll herons (basically moss-filled topiary) helps to animate the sculptures and create a pleasing tableau. The herons create a natural scene in the grass and are lightly dusted with frost, which gives the design still more character.

FIGURATIVE FORMS

The addition of a topiary piece shaped to look like some kind of animal or human figure is sure to turn some heads, but there is no reason to limit yourself to the usual menagerie of animals. You can also draw on your imagination to create something truly original.

Bizarre, even surreal figures are justifiably within the realm of topiary art and you can seek inspiration in a number of different areas, including hobbies and collections; myths and legends; films ... perhaps a child's favourite cartoon character, animal or fantasy creature.

Some shapes are only really feasible with the aid of a frame, but most can be clipped and trained freehand if you have an artistic bent. The only drawback is the time it takes for plants to grow. If you are looking for an instant effect, then moss-filled topiary, also known as "chlorophyll", is possibly the best answer.

Geometric shapes are usually created from a single type of non-variegated plant, which produces a clearly defined silhouette. But figurative forms often involve an element of fun and theatre and so the "rules" can be relaxed a little. Chlorophyll is the most flexible in this respect since you can plant into the moss with patches of differently coloured and textured foliage to correspond with different elements – the

white patches on a panda or a lion's mane, for example. It takes skill and planning to grow two different types of plant together in the traditional manner. At Walt Disney World in Florida, a topiary of Mary Poppins made from the plain green Yaupon holly (*Ilex vomitoria)* holds a parasol made from *Pyracantha coccinea*. The sun shade blossoms in spring and has red berries in autumn – just like magic! In this case, the additional element is grown as an umbrella-headed standard with the stem growing up through the main figure. Meanwhile at Sudeley Castle, in Gloucestershire, England, a lady in Tudor costume (made from an ivy-covered frame) strolls the grounds, her long train composed of a climbing rose grown from the ground up to her shoulders. The final touch is a little red book held in her hands, making her look as though she is reading.

creature features

There are certain traditional animal shapes that have always been a part of European topiary gardens. The menagerie is expanding however, and now includes exotic creatures, mythical beasts, prehistoric monsters and cartoon characters. This is thanks to the wide range of topiary frames now being offered by mail order. America leads the field in the art of moss-filled or stuffed topiary, and you'll see some of the best examples in theme parks such as Walt Disney World, in Florida. Here, giant figures, including those made more traditionally from clipped foliage, are constructed using a frame of welded steel-reinforcing rods. Some even have an internal sprinkler system that pops up like clockwork.

Frames take away the anxiety sometimes associated with clipping figurative shapes. For domestic use, frames made from 3–5mm stainless-steel rods are ideal. Because the struts of the frame are widely spaced, you can plant within and simply snip off any growth that pokes through. Sometimes you will need to select branches to train in a particular direction, though, so that they cover a particular part or extension of the frame.

It is not always practical or desirable to remove the frame once the figure has filled out, and leaving it in position rarely causes problems. If you buy ready-grown framed topiary keep an eye on those shoots that have been tied on to the frame in the initial training process, loosening or removing wire or plastic ties to prevent them cutting into the wood. Replace them with soft twine which is unlikely to cause any problems.

When choosing plants, use yew (*Taxus baccata*), box, *Ligustrum delavayanum* or shrubby honeysuckle (*Lonicera nitida*). In frost-free regions of the United States that are experiencing hot summers, yew is substituted by *Podocarpus macrophyllus* and boxwood by Yaupon holly (*Ilex vomitoria*) and forms. Reclining figures are the easiest to make quickly because you can fill out the base by planting multiples of a particular plant. Standards with a shaped head, or figures such as a ballerina balancing on one leg, take longer because you have to train the leading shoot up to the required height before pinching out the tip in order to encourage plenty of new shoots to develop above that point.

Above A snail clipped from shrubby honeysuckle (*Lonicera nitida*) makes a witty addition to a vegetable garden.

Above Before and after: this chlorophyll rabbit, perfect for a child's garden, is quick to produce using a frame.

Above Crocodiles lurk menacingly on the bank of the stream. These prone figures, planted with many small box plants, quickly fill the frame and are then simply clipped.

Left Metal frames made from stainless steel are readily available, making it easy to create chlorophyll figures. A wide range of figurative forms can be created.

Birds, such as chickens, cockerels, pheasants and peacocks, are particularly popular partly because their simple outlines are easily recognized and not out of place in the garden. These shapes are relatively easy to clip and train freehand and can guarantee good results.

how to clip a bird

1   2   3   4

1 You should start with a bushy, well-grown plant that has never been clipped before, ideally with a central stem that can be trimmed to suggest a leg. Here, we have used box (*Buxus sempervirens*), but other alternatives include privet (*Ligustrum delavayanum*) or, for speed, shrubby honeysuckle (*Lonicera nitida*). Roughly divide the foliage in half with your hands using a single stem to form the head and several stems to make the tail. Push a cane at an angle into the pot to guide the training of the head and neck. To train the stems chosen for the tail, attach a weight, a rock on a string will do, to guide them down into a gentle arc.

SUITABLE PLANTS

Buxus sempervirens (box)
Ilex (holly)
Ligustrum delavayanum
   (privet)

Lonicera nitida
Podocarpus microphyllus
Taxus baccata (yew)
Thuja

2 Begin to cut out the main shape of the bird, clipping out any of the thicker branches with secateurs (pruners). Shake out the bush as you go along to release leaves and branches that may be caught behind others.

3 Use shears to cut down into the body of the plant in order to create the curve of the back of the bird.

4 You can then shape the head and neck of the bird. To train the beak, simply twist a small length of wire around the soft wood. Continue to shape the plant, and remember to feed and water it regularly in order to encourage recovery. The ties and weights may be removed between 3 weeks to 6 months later.

Right The finished bird looks effective placed in a simple setting – here, an autumn beech hedge. The tail is beautifully silhouetted against the backdrop.

Moss-filled topiary, now termed "chlorophyll", is a great way of achieving instant results and creating a marvellous array of animals, birds and other forms. Creepers and many alpines and succulents give good results, provided that they root where they touch the moss.

how to make chlorophyll figures

1   2   3   4

1 Push your frame firmly into the ground or pot so that it is stable. If the wire is galvanized or made from stainless steel it will not rust and the sculpture will last longer.

2 Having thoroughly soaked the sphagnum moss with water, fill the frame with it, starting with the extremities. Pack in the moss tightly because when it dries out slightly it will shrink and leave gaps.

SUITABLE PLANTS

Alpine creepers and succulents e.g. *Sempervivum*

Evergreen sedges, grasses and grass-like plants

Ficus pumila (creeping fig); not hardy

Hedera helix (English ivy)

Lysimachia nummularia (creeping Jenny)

Mentha requienii (Corsican mint)

Soleirolia soleirolii (mind-your-own-business)

3 Use nylon fishing twine to wrap tightly around the frame. This helps keep the moss in place. Trim ragged pieces of moss that have escaped the binding with scissors.

4 Use a dibber or other tool in order to make holes in the moss. The moss will accommodate the rootballs of plug plants or rooted cuttings. There is no need for a complete coverage of plants because they will gradually grow and mesh together. If necessary, you can use bent "hair pins" made from florist's wire in order to fix the shoots against the moss to encourage rooting. Keep the sculpture moist, and mist drought-sensitive plants during any dry spells.

Right Some chlorophyll figures, like this life-size fishing heron wading in the margins of a pool, fit quite naturally into the garden landscape. Providing an appropriate setting or backdrop greatly enhances the effectiveness of a sculpture.

THE CUTTING EDGE

In its broadest sense, topiary is the art of shaping plants. At the cutting edge, artists experiment with topiary in a surprising number of ways, creating surreal landscapes and modern art sculptures and even moulding the ground and covering it with a living carpet of grass.

Some topiarists use traditional shapes, such as the sphere or cone, in an unconventional way, placing them in an exciting pattern or layout and mixing them with unexpected plant partners. Novel surfacing materials and even harmless spray-on dyes add a futuristic note.

Tonsile plants (that is subjects that respond well to clipping) are usually extremely malleable and with or without frames can be shaped into new and visually striking abstract forms that do not appear in the usual repertoire. Within this category are included organic, free-flowing topiaries, billowing hedging and cloud-pruned trees. Although the art of cloud pruning has been practised for centuries in the Far East, these abstract representations are nonetheless contemporary in character and work just as well in modern Western settings. Dense, clipped surfaces, so close to stone in appearance, lend themselves to being "carved" and this is another technique that designers have utilized to create interesting effects, from minimalist square panels to swirling spirals. On a much larger scale, the earth itself may be carved or moulded into abstract shapes and symbols. Elements such as labyrinths and grassed amphitheatres make dramatic, yet low-maintenance features for larger spaces. At the other end of the spectrum in small plots, simply mowing or clipping lawn grass to different lengths, thereby creating intriguing temporary patterns, is something that even a novice could master.

On the fringe, artists create patterned carpets created by slotting together contrasting plant materials. Drought-resistant greenery in modular or stacking honeycomb planters can be used to landscape a bare wall and versatile ivy is the perfect material for creating patterns on a wall.

Right At the avant-garde Chaumont festival, structures that are reminiscent of Venetian gondolas carry patterned plantings through the rising mist.

cloud topiary

Though normally associated with Japanese gardens, cloud topiary is found throughout the Far East and is equally a part of traditional Chinese and Thai gardens. There are numerous, subtly different forms of cloud topiary, but, as the name suggests, they all involve the foliage being clipped into cloud-like shapes.

Choose your plant depending on the size of specimen required. A dainty, potted, cloud-pruned shrub can be grown from one of the many forms of Japanese holly (*Ilex crenata*), Yaupon holly (*Ilex vomitoria*), which is a native of south-eastern North America, box or the small-leaved privet (*Ligustrum delavayanum*). For quick results, you could also experiment

with the shrubby honeysuckle (*Lonicera nitida*) or one of the many junipers, most of which have attractive, peeling bark. For larger specimens, conifers such as Japanese cedar (*Cryptomeria japonica*), Japanese black pine (*Pinus thunbergii*) and *Pinus sylvestris* 'Watereri' are ideal.

Unlike many topiary shapes, the training of cloud-pruned specimens invariably uses a reasonably mature plant. It is important to pick your specimen with care, looking beneath the foliage for an interesting formation of branches because they'll be an important, visible feature. Multi-stemmed subjects work best, and the more gnarled and twisted the branches the better the

how to make a cloud topiary

Choose a shrub such as box (*Buxus sempervirens*), Japanese holly (*Ilex crenata*) or other small-leaved evergreens. Large specimens from garden centres are likely to be expensive,

so it is worth looking in your garden to see if you have a suitable plant, particularly if this is your first attempt at topiary. Look for a shrub with a good "bone" structure.

1 Open up the foliage with both hands in order to reveal the framework of branches. An ideal scenario is one or more main stems with strong side branches.

2 Cut out any unwanted branches leaving behind more than you will actually need at this stage. Turn the plant around and stand back regularly to see the shape.

3 Strip the leaves and smaller branches off the main stems that are to be retained. Use bamboo canes and wire to bend some branches to shape.

4 Trim the other branches at the stem tips to encourage compact growth. There should be space between each "cloud". Clip once or twice in spring and summer.

result. Though there are some more stylized forms of cloud topiary, originally the idea was to create the look of an ancient, wind-blown mountain pine growing out of a rock crevice. When placing plants, take advantage of any with a pronounced lean which might work well arcing over a pond or stretch of gravel.

Begin by removing all the foliage and small side branches from the main stems that you have decided to keep. But do retain the growth towards the ends of the branches because this will later be shaped into clouds, ranging from flattened plates to globes. The foliage clipping and shaping uses traditional topiary techniques. Though cloud topiary is usually asymmetric, occasionally you'll see trees with a single main stem and relatively short, alternately stepped side branches. Stem shape is trained with bamboo canes.

Above This cloud-pruned tree, arcing over the water, appears to have been sculpted by the elements over centuries.

Left A topiarist at Le Parc Oriental near the Loire Valley, in France, trims one of the larger trees.

Below *Ilex crenata*, the Japanese holly, is ideal for creating smaller cloud-pruned trees for containers.

surface patterns

The dense, evenly clipped surface of formal hedging or large topiary pieces can be cut to create patterns in relief. The finer the detail required, the smaller the leaf must be. Plants such as box, yew and other conifers, and the shrubby honeysuckle (*Lonicera nitida*), are ideal, especially if they have been regularly cut to create an evenly branched surface layer. The process is much like carving a piece of masonry.

The ideal time to cut is when the surface is resprouting after its last clipping; that way the design will stand out more clearly. One of the most impressive displays of such topiary can be found at the Clipsham Yew Walk, in Rutland, England, where an avenue of yews has been clipped to include a variety of motifs and emblems, including regimental coats of arms.

Above Trained over a simple framework, ivy can be used to create simple geometric designs or figurative forms.

how to make a surface pattern

Define motifs such as a series of square-, rectangular- or diamond-shaped panels in a clipped vertical surface by cutting a groove around a template held with tape. Modern patterns include spirals and Celtic symbols.

1 The undulating form of this hedge suggested an Egyptian eye to the artist. The outer shape was defined with hand shears and the region of the eye itself lightly trimmed to act as a guide.

2 A shallow, v-shaped groove was cut around the eye and then the pupil was made by snipping out a circular depression. Any bare stems will soon recover but the shape will need regular clipping.

Use secateurs (pruners), sheep shears or small hand shears to provide greater control and precision cutting. Although shallow cuts inevitably disappear quite quickly, this is a fun way to experiment with sculpting. Do not worry if the cuts expose an interior of bare branches. Provided the plant is one that regenerates readily – for example yew or box – it will soon be covered in new leaves.

Fruit trees (such as apples and pears) can be pruned and trained against a wall to create ornamental espaliers with tiers of horizontal branches and you can create a similar look with woody shrubs like Japanese quince (*Chaenomeles*) and *Pyracantha* (firethorn) whose berry crop is more prominently displayed. You can also train vigorous plants across a house wall, removing or bending all outward-pointing new shoots into the supporting wires so that they create a smooth covering or second skin. Neatly training the new growth around windows and doors highlights the architectural features. Good subjects include *Cotoneaster horizontalis*, *Euonymus fortunei* 'Silver Queen' and compact evergreen climbers such as star jasmine (*Trachelospermum jasminoides*).

The use of architectural *treillage* panels which are mounted on wall battens is another excellent way of training and shaping plants such as ivy. You can use the panels as a 2-D topiary frame in order to create a pattern such as a series of arches. Once these have been covered by foliage, trim off excess shoots around the edges of the frame.

Ivy is also ideal for creating more fluid shapes because it is evergreen and self-clinging, and responds well to clipping. Make a template for your design using plastic-coated trellis mesh. Plain green forms of English ivy (*Hedera helix*) work well but if a larger leaf is required, try Persian ivy (*Hedera colchica* 'Dentata').

Above The design of this planted wall of dwarf box and cotton lavender (*Santolina*) is based on a simple parterre.

Above A box hedge clipped in a billowing, go-with-the-flow form bears raised surface patterns reminiscent of ancient petroglyphs or rock carvings. Simple designs such as this are most effective.

organic form

One of the most radical developments in European topiary in recent years has been the introduction of free-flowing, organic shapes. This style of naturalistic contouring is striking when contrasted with crisp architectural elements, such as formal pools and the walls of buildings, but it also works well as textured groundcover in more relaxed or less intensively cultivated areas.

While the Eastern influence is obvious, and the similarity to cloud pruning undeniable, this approach is adaptable and in keeping with modern trends and New Age approaches to gardening, such as feng shui. Few people have had more influence in popularizing the technique and demonstrating its potential than the designers Jacques and Peter Wirtz.

At home you can have great fun experimenting and just seeing what shapes emerge and, if you have a mature and perhaps slightly overgrown shrub border or unruly mixed hedge, you could begin clipping right away. But to achieve a more uniform look in terms of texture and colour, it is advisable to start from scratch, planting in blocks of one subject.

The plants can be clipped separately, giving a bumpy basket-of-eggs shape, but it is more usual to allow them to fuse, thereby creating an undulating surface of mini hills and valleys. Box is the perfect material because, even when left untouched, it develops a soft, cloud-like profile that is easily accentuated. Also, despite its reputation for slow growth, it can reach substantial proportions. The beauty of box trained in this naturalistic manner can be seen in gardens – some around 200 years old – across the eastern coast of North America. Here scores of different box cultivars are grown but, until relatively recently, formal geometric training of box was frowned upon and largely confined to the historic colonial gardens.

One of the most commonly planted cultivars of common box in the United States is dwarf box (*Buxus sempervirens* 'Suffruticosa'), known there as English box. In formal European gardens it is trimmed to create low edging, knots and parterres, but in the United States it is allowed to grow almost unrestricted, producing undulating groundcover, surprisingly tall hedges and garden divides. Maintenance consists of thinning to allow more light and air into the interior and some light clipping. Other plants include small-leaved evergreens, like some cotoneasters, shrubby honeysuckle (*Lonicera nitida*) and Japanese azaleas.

Left These rolling mounds of creeping bamboo are punctuated by carefully placed rocks to create a natural-looking, miniature landscape.

Right Organic topiary takes many forms and some designs seamlessly combine classic geometric elements with rounded or undulating shapes to create highly original results.

land art

During the 1960s and '70s a disparate group of artists began exploring ways of using the landscape as a canvas for their work. Some pieces were ephemeral, utilizing whatever natural materials came to hand in order to create patterns on the ground, but, in one branch of the Land Art Movement (as it became known), the ground itself was shaped and contoured on a large scale using a bulldozer, with the resulting "landforms" being covered in grass. Today, at the beginning of the 21st century, these turf-covered creations are again increasingly finding their way into private gardens as well as open, public spaces.

Garden earthworks are by no means a new idea. Grassy viewing mounds were found in medieval gardens and, during the Elizabethan period, more complex designs appeared including symbolic snail or spiral mounts. Much later, during the 18th century, exponents of the Landscape Movement set about restructuring the natural profile of the land to create more interesting vistas. Well-defined geometric structures were also created including, for example, a huge turf amphitheatre carved into the side of a hill at Claremont, in Surrey. Such substantial edifices are even more remarkable because they were dug entirely by hand. Though we tend to view Land Art as

Above Land-art features such as this stepped mound can transform a flat, open area of the garden and create much needed contrast in levels.

Left In this stunning piece of terracing it is almost as though a construction of stone has been overlaid and softened by a carpet of turf. Take care when designing land-art elements that the piece can be maintained fairly easily.

relatively modern, the work of some contemporary designers brings to mind ancient earthworks, such as Neolithic burial mounds and raised, Iron Age forts.

The inspiration for the varied contours ranges from the aesthetic to the spiritual and symbolic. One contemporary exponent, architectural historian Charles Jenks, even based his structures on the chaos theory and patterns of fractal geometry. So, today's earthworks may have broad curving or swirling lines, or be shaped like a pyramid or ziggurat (an ancient pyramidal temple-tower). They may even reflect or complement the landscape or mimic natural features. For example, you could create a series of tapering mounds like distant hills. Whatever the shape, the structure has to be well-compacted to make it stable, especially considering that it may be formed from several hundred tonnes of soil. To maintain high-quality turf, you may need to install automatic irrigation and slopes should not be steeper than about 45 degrees to facilitate mowing. Ground contoured with rocks and soil in the naturalistic setting of a Japanese tea garden, for example, can be softened with mosses and plants like *Soleirolia soleirolii*.

Above In the heart of the London suburbs is a Japanese-inspired water garden with organically sculpted banks that has been designed as a miniature representation of a snaking river valley.

Left Acting as a giant piece of abstract art, the wave-like contours of this earth bank, supported in places by timber, are planted with turf and – on the steeper sides that are prone to drying out – with sedums. The latter tolerate shade and drought.

turf sculpting

Grass might not be the first plant you'd think of in association with topiary, but humble turf can actually be transformed into a variety of ornamental features. Take the lawn, for example. On a subtle level, mowing in more than one direction using a mower with a roller can produce more attractive patterns than simple stripes. Knowing how the sun moves around the garden is a big advantage. For example, a second oblique cut, invisible

for part of the day, will be lit up when the sun moves into position to highlight this set of stripes, leading the eye in a completely different direction across the garden.

Mowing sweeping curves and other patterns on the lawn by cutting sections to different lengths can also be great fun – like painting abstract shapes on a giant canvas. Raise or lower the cutting height between adjacent sections, or leave areas of the

Above Looking like they have just emerged from underground, a table and set of turf stools makes an imaginative and easily constructed piece of garden art. This type of turf sculpting is perfect for children to play on.

Right This circular feature, which centres on a small ornamental tree, brings to mind a turf labyrinth. However, closer inspection reveals that the contours are created by using alternating bands of grass mown at different heights.

lawn uncut for one or two sessions while the rest of the grass is mown. Lawn sculpting is easy to modify or eradicate if you get tired of the design.

One easy motif that is well worth trying is the spiral. Start by mowing or shearing inside the rim of a circle, gradually moving inwards towards the centre, leaving a strip of unmown grass to highlight the route. Children love running along the track, treating it like a miniature maze. If you are a fan of the surreal, then you can also create your own permanent outdoor furniture using turf as a fabric. For example, an

armchair with a cardboard frame is available on the Internet. Once in position you simply fill the spaces with soil and sow with grass seed.

Turf sculpture is created by first moulding the soil, just as you might have as a child making figures out of sand. These are then sown with grass seed. What could be more bizarre than clothes created from turf? This is not exactly everyday wear, but several costume designers and performance artists have made and worn such creations. The grass seed is sown onto jute matting, no soil is involved, but you must remember to water every day!

green weaving

Willow (or withy) sculpture is now a popular form of garden art. If you are using seasoned willow sticks or wands you'll have to pre-soak them to make them pliable. The advantage of using fresh willow is that stems are cut after leaf fall, through late autumn and winter – the perfect time for taking hardwood cuttings. When pushed into the ground to make the structure stable, the withies invariably root to give even better anchorage and in spring the structure will begin to show signs of life, before long being peppered with narrow leaves.

There are numerous sculptural forms that can be created, ranging from magical green bowers to decorative living screens which are easy to construct. To make one of the latter with an attractive diamond pattern, simply insert the wands diagonally in the ground – half in one direction and half in the other and then weave the stems under and over, creating the pattern as you go. Finally, trim the top and ends of the panel and fasten off to secure the framework. For a long, arched tunnel, set two parallel rows of wands in the ground and bend the ends over to meet or overlap in the middle. Weave horizontal pieces along the length of each side for added strength. A snaking structure is great fun for children, as well as providing a flowing, abstract feature to relieve an expanse of grass, for example.

Several types of willow (*Salix*) are used and, depending on the species, the bark colour ranges from olive green to gold, flame red or purple. The common osier (*Salix viminalis*) is ideal for larger pieces, such as arbours and tunnels. For coloured stems try forms

Left By weaving live willow wands set into the ground, you can create living screens like this simple diamond design. Trim the regrowth hard back.

Right Small-leaved ivies (*Hedera helix* cultivars) are perfect for covering wooden *treillage*. The plants form a softer version of the screen, but must be trimmed to maintain the underlying form.

of *S. alba*, such as the red willow (*S. a.* subsp. *vitellina* 'Britzensis') or violet willow (*S. daphnoides*), and for fences and screens try the grey sallow (*S. cinerea*). The willows are stooled or coppiced to generate a mass of straight, smooth wands.

With the proliferation of willow-weaving courses at craft and conservation centres, it is now reasonably easy to obtain bundles of fresh willow stems or buy direct from specialist companies. Although willow thrives on damp, heavy ground it by no means requires moisture. When growing your own, take care to site plants sensibly as almost all species have invasive root systems that can interfere with drains and the foundations of buildings.

Right A woven willow arbour will sprout a mass of new shoots each spring, giving it a distinctly rustic character that would suit a cottage or country garden.

TOPIARY
PLANTS

Most of the plants in this section share key characteristics. On clipping, the ideal topiary plant will become more densely branched with smaller leaves, resulting in a smooth-textured appearance without unsightly gaps. When cut back hard, either for formative work or during restoration, woody growth should regenerate easily.

Choosing the right plant is essential to the success of your project and the directory lists the relative merits of each of the more popular subjects, but also includes details on more unusual plants that could broaden your horizons.

You will find a preponderance of evergreen species and cultivars because topiary and green architecture should have a year-round presence. However, some vigorous deciduous species have been included, since these can make substantial structural elements, such as tall hedges and pleached screens, relatively quickly. Tough, deciduous plants may be preferable in exposed gardens or those experiencing harsh winters.

Left It is advisable to choose those plants that are best suited to particular forms of topiary, such as cloud pruning, or which fit the scale of the garden or outdoor space concerned.

caring for your plants

TOOLS AND EQUIPMENT

The different pieces of equipment that you will need when topiarizing will very much depend on the type and scale of topiary that you are planning.

The more expensive tools tend to have blades made out of harder steel, which does not blunt as quickly. Proper maintenance will prolong the life of your equipment and includes sharpening as well as cleaning and oiling blades after use to prevent rust.

Secateurs (pruners) Use secateurs to trim thin woody stems and soft shoots as well as to shape and maintain large-leaved evergreen topiaries. Bypass secateurs cut more cleanly than anvil types, which can squash or bruise the stems. Left-handed types are available and ratchet pruners allow tough stems to be cut in stages without straining your hand.

Long-handled pruners These have more leverage than secateurs, and therefore more cutting power. Use them to cut through thicker stems. Ones with

Above The flame creeper (*Tropaeolum speciosum*) is a traditional partner for yew, the herbaceous growth doing little harm.

telescopic handles have a greater reach. Do not overstrain – move to a small pruning saw with a curved blade if the branch is too thick to cut through easily.

Shears These are available in different sizes. The smallest, often labelled ladies' shears, have short blades and a narrow "snout", and are essential for any kind of detailed clipping and shaping. Hedge- cutting shears, with wavy-edged blades, are designed to resist clogging and these are ideal for maintaining large, simple topiary forms. Do not try to clip tough stems with small shears as you risk damaging the blades. Also ensure that the blades of any shears are regularly sharpened. Clean off the sticky sap from the blades as you work. One-handed shears are useful for light trimming. Those such as sheep shears are often sold in connection with topiary, but, as with all one-handed shears and pruners, prolonged use can be tiring.

Hedgetrimmers Electric, petrol- driven or battery operated, hedgetrimmers are powered by a range of motors and have different blade lengths. The more powerful petrol-driven models suit gardens with a lot of formal hedging or large topiary shapes to maintain, and are useful where there is no convenient power supply. Electric models are lighter and may be less tiring to work with. Battery operated models have increased in power over recent years and are a good viable option where there is no electricity available.

Rest the equipment to avoid burning out the motor and do not tackle material that is too thick for the blades to cut with ease. Clean the blades and replenish the lubricant as required.

Above Areas of damage caused by mechanical injury, pests or diseases should be cut out to allow healthy wood to regenerate.

PLANT MAINTENANCE

After spending so much time designing and creating your topiary specimens, you will want to ensure that they are well kept and maintained. Feeding, clipping, repair work and winter protection are all tasks that may need to be undertaken at some stage.

Clipping Check the topiary plants directory on the following pages for ideal timings for clipping. For evergreens, this is generally in spring or early summer, after the risk of frost has passed, and again in late summer, which gives any re-growth time to toughen up before the winter. Cutting too early or too late can promote lots of soft, vulnerable shoots that are liable to be scorched by frost and cold winds. Be aware of any potential nesting birds in hedges and larger topiary pieces. If there is a chance that birds might be nesting avoid any clipping between 1st March and 31st August.

Trim most deciduous plants in the dormant period, but clip spring- and early-summer-flowering standards that bloom on the previous season's growth immediately after flowering to give the new wood time to mature.

When clipping rounded shapes, turn the shears over so that the blade follows the curve more easily. If you are unsure about how close to trim, just clip over lightly, removing some of the re-growth and then stand back to assess your progress. Do not be afraid to switch to secateurs (pruners) or sheep shears if you feel that you do not have enough control.

Before trimming hedging, including parterres and knots, put down ground sheets to collect debris. The removal of clippings helps to prevent disease problems.

Feeding Large topiaries grown in a lawn may not need feeding if the grass is regularly treated with fertilizer. A slow-release granular fertilizer, designed for shrubs and roses, and raked in around the base of your topiary pieces in spring is ideal for border plants. The shallow roots of box can be damaged causing foliage scorching so instead mulch with garden compost or manure.

Potted topiary Pick a pot that easily accommodates the root system but which is in proportion with the top growth or frame. For long-term container planting, use a soil-based potting mix, perhaps mixed with some peat-free potting mix to lighten the composition. Cover the drainage holes with crocks or broken pots and/or several inches of coarse gravel to allow excess water to escape. Leave sufficient gap between the soil surface and the rim of the pot to facilitate watering. Apply liquid feed between mid- to late spring and late summer, and water regularly. Routinely turn pots set against a wall so that they receive even light. Top up with fresh potting mix every spring in order to cover over any roots that have been exposed where watering has eroded the soil.

Renovation and repair Plants can become threadbare or die back in patches, often because of a lack of light or problems with pests and diseases. If the rest of the plant is healthy, cut out all the dead branches and, if necessary, open out the hole to allow in more light. This, combined with feeding and watering, should encourage the dormant buds to sprout and fill in the damage.

When old plants get out of shape or fail to produce much new growth, it could mean that they need to be rejuvenated. This involves cutting hard back into the framework of branches.

Winter protection Ideally, move potted topiary within the sheltered environs of the house (e.g. against a warm wall) or, for tender species, under glass. Wrap pots left outdoors with layers of bubble plastic insulation to protect the roots and use horticultural fleece to cover the foliage of types vulnerable to wind scorch. For standards, use foam pipe insulation or lagging to protect the stem from frost. Ensure good winter drainage by raising up pots on feet or wheeled bases.

Above Choose shade-tolerant plants such as box or yew where shade from overhanging trees is likely to be a problem.

Above These impressive yew pyramids will lose their shaggy appearance when they are clipped over with a hedgetrimmer. They make a striking and statuesque backdrop for this unusual bench seat.

a-z of topiary plants

Buxus
BOX

Shrubby evergreen invaluable for topiary with small leaves and a dense branching habit. *Buxus sempervirens* has scores of different forms but the species, common box or boxwood, is the most widely used for topiary.

Cultivation Box enjoys slightly alkaline, humus-rich soil and grows well in shade, disliking hot, dry conditions. Pot plants are best fed with dilute liquid feed, while those in the ground thrive with an annual mulch of well-rotted horse manure or garden compost. This helps retain moisture in the soil and provides nutrients. Do not top-dress with concentrated granular fertilizer as the surface roots will burn. Clip in late spring or early summer and again before the end of late summer.

Use glazed pots instead of terracotta because they keep the roots cool and moist. Also use pots whose width exceeds their depth to accommodate the surface roots. When planting a hedge or using several plants to construct a shape, use identical clones, otherwise variations will spoil the effect.

Varieties So-called dwarf box (*B. sempervirens* 'Suffruticosa'; hardy/Z 6–9), is commonly used for creating knots and parterres and for edging paths. Another frequently used plant for knots and parterres is the compact *B. microphylla* 'Faulkner'. Hardier alternatives include the slow-growing *B. sempervirens* 'Vardar Valley', *B. sinica* var. *insularis* (hardy/Z 4–9) and *B. microphylla* 'Compacta' (hardy/Z 5–9). Variegated forms include the cream-marbled *B. sempervirens* 'Elegantissima'. Some forms of *B. microphylla*, such as 'Green Pillow', produce a pleasing shape with little training.

Uses Modest hedges; figurative and geometric shapes, including those requiring fine detail; standards; free-form clipping; knots and parterres.

Problems Box blight *Cylindrocladium buxicola* is a fungal disease which results in bare patches and die-back of box leaves. *Volutella* is another blight that affects box but not so seriously. All varieties of box are susceptible. Although there is no cure for box blight, the Royal Horticultural Society website (www.rhs.org.uk) have a series of excellent pages on diagnosis and treatment recommendations.

Box *psyllid* is an insect that causes apical buds to distort and resemble tiny Brussels sprouts. It is not usually serious and can be controlled by clipping, blasting the plants with strong jets of water or spraying in mid-spring with insecticidal soap.

Reddish-brown leaves usually signify stress, such as cold conditions, not enough feed, or excess heat.

Carpinus betulus
COMMON HORNBEAM

Sometimes confused with beech, common hornbeam (*Carpinus betulus*) is a deciduous shrub with broad green leaves. It holds onto its autumn leaves through the winter, making it an ideal choice for formal hedges. It can be pleached or trained over a framework of *treillage*.

Cultivation Hornbeam is weather-resistant and hardy, and grows on most soils in sun or light shade. Prune in early and late summer.

Varieties Common hornbeam (*C. betulus*) and the upright *C. b.* 'Fastigiata'. (Hardy/Z 5–9)

Uses Formal hedging and other large architectural elements, including stilt hedges and pleached screens; tunnels or *berceaux*.

Problems Few

Chamaecyparis
CYPRESS

The familiar hedging conifer, lawson cypress (*Chamaecyparis lawsoniana*), is a vigorous grower, often utilized as a windbreak especially near the coast.

Cultivation Best on humus-rich, moisture-retentive, alkaline soil. Clip at least twice a year during the growing period (in spring and late summer outside nesting), but do not cut back too hard into brown growth because new shoots rarely regenerate from old wood.

Varieties A range of foliage colours; there are slower-growing forms with a conical habit. (Hardy/Z 6–9)

Uses Geometric figures, large architectural elements and hedges.

Problems Few

Cotoneaster

The small-leaved evergreen, semi-evergreen or deciduous types of prostrate or dome-forming cotoneasters are best. Deciduous *Cotoneaster horizontalis* has structured, fishbone-like branches as well as good autumn leaf colour and usually excellent berries.

Cultivation Hardy and easy to grow, tolerates clay but prefers free-draining soil. Full sun is best but it grows in partial shade. Prune deciduous and semi-evergreen forms in winter. *C. microphyllus* is best clipped after the profusion of tiny white blooms has faded and, again, in late summer (though you will lose some berries) or clip in alternate years.

Varieties *C. horizontalis* (hardy/Z 5–9) will cover a north- or east-facing wall. For a tight, close-knit form, use the bushy, dome-shaped *C. microphyllus* (hardy/Z 6–8).

Uses *C. horizontalis* gives semi-formal wall coverage; *C. microphyllus* makes formal domes as well as free-form shapes. Some cotoneasters are trained to make small, weeping standards.

Problems Few

Buxus sempervirens

Buxus sempervirens 'Elegantissima'

Buxus sempervirens 'Marginata'

Chamaecyparis

Crataegus
HAWTHORN

Common hawthorn (*Crataegus monogyna*), as well as *C. laevigata*, grow into thorny, deciduous shrubs or small trees which, when left untrimmed, have creamy white blossom in late spring and red autumn fruit. Although now used chiefly as a boundary hedging plant in rural cottage gardens, hawthorn was once prized as a topiary plant and used in formal gardens long before yew came into vogue.
Cultivation Extremely hardy and wind resistant, it will grow on most soils including heavy clay. Clip during the dormant period.
Varieties *C. monogyna* (hardy/ Z 5–7); *C. laevigata* (hardy/Z 5–8) has several forms with pink or red, double or single blooms.
Uses As a semi-formal hedge with a rounded top; is an excellent deterrent to intruders. Frequently trained into arches, but tricky to shape into forms that require fine detail or crisp geometry; makes characterful, dome-headed standards.

x Cupressocyparis leylandii
LEYLAND CYPRESS

Loathed by some because of its reputation for growing far too tall and blocking out the light, leyland cypress is a gift for impatient topiarists wishing to make large architectural structures in a hurry. If clipped frequently, it develops a dense, fine-textured appearance.
Cultivation Easily established on most neutral to acid soils, except

those that are waterlogged or very dry. Clip frequently when in active growth, but do not cut into brown foliage as old wood rarely regrows.
Varieties Gold-leaved forms, such as 'Castlewellan', 'Gold Rider' and 'Robinson's Gold', are less vigorous than × *Cupressocyparis leylandii*. (Hardy/Z 6–9)
Uses Formal hedging and wind-breaks as well as architectural shapes including green colonnades, arches and *exedrae*. With care, hedges may be kept to just 30cm (12in) wide. Golden varieties are sometimes used for large, corkscrew spirals.
Problems With poor growing conditions, it is susceptible to fungal diseases such as cankers and soil-borne *Phytophthora*. Hedging plants purchased from nurseries may be pot bound, adversely affecting establishment. Avoid plants over 45cm (18in) tall.

Cupressus
CYPRESS

These large coniferous trees have a conical habit and look statuesque and elegant in the garden.
Cultivation Arizona cypress (*Cupressus arizonica*; hardy/Z 7–9) prefers light, free-draining soil. The fast-growing Monterey cypress (*C. macrocarpa*) tolerates sea spray, and makes a good specimen in mild coastal gardens. The Italian cypress (*C. sempervirens*) is hardier than its reputation suggests, and can be grown in cold-climate gardens. Stake trees for the first few years to assist root development.

Varieties *C. macrocarpa* (hardy/ Z 7–10) is vigorous with bright green foliage and has a number of gold-leaved forms which require full sun to develop the best colour. Also try *C. m.* 'Goldcrest' (conical with bright lime-green foliage); fastigiate forms of *C. sempervirens* (frost hardy/ Z 8–10), such as 'Green Pencil', and members of the Stricta Group, are slim and upright.
Uses Arizona cypress is often trained into triple-ball standards and corkscrews; Italian cypress is used as a strong vertical accent or for formal avenues, and Monterey cypress for close-grained, green architectural shapes.
Problems May lean or fall over if the root system is not well developed.

Euonymus
SPINDLE TREE

Evergreen forms of euonymus are useful and colourful topiary plants. They are salt and pollution tolerant, while *Euonymus fortunei* cultivars are tough, often developing pink tints after a frost. The white-variegated forms can be grown in shade and do not revert to all-green.
Cultivation Plants are easily grown on most well-drained soils. Avoid planting *E. japonicus* types in cold, frost-prone areas.
Varieties *E. fortunei* cultivars (hardy/ Z 5–9) ,such as the variegated 'Silver Queen', 'Emerald 'n' Gold' and 'Emerald Gaiety'. *E. japonicus* (frost hardy/Z 7–10) and cultivars vary from the dwarf 'Microphyllus' forms to the larger- leaved, bushy cultivars, such as 'Aureus' and 'Ovatus Aureus'.

Uses Small-leaved forms of *E. fortunei*, as well as 'Microphyllus' forms of *E. japonicus*, can be clipped to form low hedging. *E. f.* 'Silver Queen' and large-leaved forms of *E. japonicus* make excellent clipped domes. 'Silver Queen' also makes a good wall covering. In mild areas, *E. japonicus* is used as a glossy-leaved, medium-sized hedging plant. Small-leaved *E. fortunei* cultivars can be trained as small potted standards.
Problems Scale insect. Leaf notching by adult vine weevils.
Frost damage on spring growth of *E. japonicus*. Watch for all-green reversions on variegated plants.

Fagus sylvatica
EUROPEAN BEECH

A robust and relatively fast-growing hedging plant, it has broad, mid-green leaves that turn copper in autumn and last all winter. It contrasts strikingly with evergreen yew.
Cultivation Full sun to part shade. Grows on any soil that is well drained, including alkaline. Trimming or pruning in late summer to avoid bird nesting also encourages good autumn leaf coverage.
Varieties *Fagus sylvatica* has many forms, including purple leaf, fastigiate and weeping cultivars. American beech (*F. grandifolia*) has similar uses to European beech, but prefers acidic soil. (Hardy/Z 4–7)
Uses Suitable for formal boundary hedges and screens, and features such as arches, tunnels and *exedrae* as well as broad pyramids.
Problems Few, though can suffer from aphid attack.

× *Cupressocyparis leylandii* 'Golconda'

Euonymus fortunei 'Emerald 'n' Gold'

Euonymus variegata 'Silver Queen'

Fagus sylvatica

Hebe

An evergreen New Zealand native. The many small-leaved species make dense, low domes in the wild; light clipping enhances the shape.

Cultivation Salt and wind tolerant, the small-leaved hebes are ideal for seaside gardens, but, with good frost protection, also perform well in cities. Grow on any well-drained soil in full sun. Between late spring and midsummer clip lightly with shears, taking off just a few centimetres of soft shoot growth. Plants that have been damaged can be rejuvenated by cutting back some of the branches to just above the point where new shoots are sprouting at the base.

Varieties *Hebe rakaiensis* has light olive-green leaves; *H.* 'Red Edge' is light grey with a pink rim; *H. topiaria* is bright green, and forms a tight bun shape with little clipping. (Hardy/Z 8)

Uses Plant the dome shapes in a grid pattern to create a surface texture; use in a mixed border.

Problems In cold winters plants may be damaged by frost. Unless clipped annually foliage can develop gaps.

Hedera helix
COMMON IVY, ENGLISH IVY

With hundreds of cultivars, the range of leaf shape and variegation is staggering. *Hedera helix* has very flexible stems, making it ideal for growing over 3-D frames; it roots where it touches damp moss, hence its popularity for chlorophyll figures. Plain green cultivars are best for geometric shapes that mimic traditional topiary.

Cultivation Plain green cultivars thrive in deep shade, but the more variegation, the more light is required. Drought tolerant when established, ivy prefers well-drained soil or potting mix. Wind the stems around supports and snip off excess growth; shearing is possible when grown over large topiary frames.

Varieties Choose small-leaved types of *H. helix* (hardy/Z 5–9 unless stated otherwise) with short joints (the space between the leaves), such as 'Duckfoot' or 'Très Coupé', which provide even coverage on small to medium-sized figures. Use faster-growing forms, such as 'Green Ripple' (frost hardy/Z 8–9), for swags and garlands. 'Glacier' (frost hardy/Z 8–9) has silver-white mottling and lightens a shady wall. Compact, brightly variegated forms – 'Eva' (frost hardy/Z 8–9), 'Kolibri' and 'Little Diamond' – create contrasting areas on moss-filled animal figures. *Hedera hibernica* 'Deltoidea' (hardy/Z 5–9) grows flat and even, and is useful for wall patterns such as covering trellis shapes.

Uses For 3-D topiary frames (quick substitutes for geometric forms); for moss-filled or chlorophyll figures (either planted in the pot or directly into the moss); for wall decoration, trained free-hand or on wires; for creating swags and garlands.

Problems Under hot dry conditions, ivy is susceptible to spider mite. Spraying with water, as well as a cool shady position, help keep it at bay. Check potting mix for vine weevils. When old framed topiary becomes woody and threadbare, replant.

Hyssopus
HYSSOP

Traditionally used in knot gardens, this aromatic herb (bushy evergreen or semi-evergreen) is used to make low hedges, either flat-topped or rounded. The foliage is dark green, glossy and needle-like and has spikes of blue blooms from midsummer.

Cultivation Tolerates thin, limey soils but must have good drainage and full sun. Clip either in midsummer or spring. Only cut back the new soft growth, not the woody base.

Varieties Herb nurseries should stock forms of *Hyssopus officinalis* with coloured flowers. (Hardy/Z 6–9)

Uses Low hedges and edging, knots and small domes.

Problems Can get rather leggy with age. Discard threadbare plants.

Ilex
HOLLY

Many hollies are used for topiary and green architecture, and these evergreen shrubs or trees offer plain green or brightly variegated foliage to suit every size of garden. Berries are borne on female forms provided a male pollinator is nearby. Japanese (*Ilex crenata*) and Yaupon (*I. vomitoria*) hollies have very small leaves and closely resemble box.

Cultivation Grows in any reasonable soil. Plain green forms of common holly (*I. aquifolium*) and Highclere holly (*I.* x *altaclerensis*) are very shade tolerant. *I. crenata* 'Golden Gem' needs full sun to develop its yellow leaves. Ideally, shape large-leaved hollies with secateurs (pruners) or long-handled pruners rather than hedge trimmers to avoid half-cut leaves. Prune in spring and again in late summer if necessary.

Varieties *I. aquifolium* and forms (frost hardy/Z 7), such as 'Handsworth New Silver' (cream-and-pink variegation); 'J. C. van Tol' (green-leaved hedging); 'Pyramidalis' (compact upright cone); *I.* x *altaclerensis* (frost hardy/Z 7–9) and forms similar to *I. aquifolium*, such as 'Golden King' (female; bright gold variegation and red berries). Compact, slow-growing hollies include *I. crenata* (hardy/Z 6–8) and *I. c.* 'Golden Gem', *I. vomitoria* (Yaupon; hardy/Z 8–10) and, for dwarf hedging, *I. vomitoria* 'Nana' (hardy/ Z 4–9).

Uses Forms of common and Highclere holly are used for hedging and large architectural features, as well as geometric specimens, such as cones, obelisks, mushroom-headed trees, cake stands and ball-headed standards. The latter may be grown in pots. Japanese holly makes small domes but can be cloud pruned or shaped into free-flowing forms. In America, the native Yaupon is a substitute for box in regions with hot summers, being clipped into shapes or used for hedging.

Problems Few, though common holly can be quite temperamental if cut back hard. Beware fallen leaves of prickly specimens when weeding.

Juniperus
JUNIPER

These wind- and drought-tolerant hardy conifers may not be your first choice for topiary, but *Juniperus*

Hedera helix 'Green Ripple'

Hyssopus officinalis

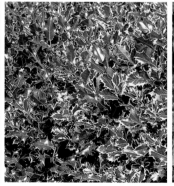
Ilex aquifolium cultivar

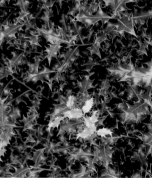
Ilex aquifolium cultivar

communis was once commonly used for topiary. Several different species and forms are used, offering a variety of foliage colours, including blues, greys, bright greens and gold. Some slender, upright varieties need little maintenance to keep their shape. Junipers tolerate clipping better than many conifers, and can regrow from old wood.

Cultivation Grows on any free-draining soil; tolerates lime but must have full sun. Clip during late spring or summer.

Varieties *J. communis* (hardy/Z 3–7) and forms, such as the columnar *J. c.* 'Hibernica'; *J. chinensis* (hardy/Z 5–9) *and J. pfitzeriana* 'Mint Julep' (hardy/Z 4–9).

Uses Round-headed standards; triple balls; corkscrews; hedges in exposed gardens; columns; cloud topiary.

Problems Few

Laburnum

The late spring or early summer flowering laburnums are well known for their bright yellow flowers. These fast-growing trees have soft, pliable young stems, making them easy to train over a framework. *Laburnum alpinum* 'Pendulum' produces pods of poisonous seeds which can be a danger to children, so try the safer *L.* x *watereri* 'Vossii' which has long, pea-like flowers. The foliage of both is light green and divided into leaflets.

Cultivation Easily grown in full sun. Tie to a framework and remove excess growth as required.

Varieties *L. alpinum* 'Pendulum' (hardy/Z 5–8), but better to choose

L. x *watereri* 'Vossii' (hardy/Z 6–8) which flowers slightly later and has much longer blooms that cascade down through struts.

Uses Tunnels.

Problems None, provided you use *L.* x *watereri* 'Vossii' which does not set seed.

Laurus

BAY LAUREL, SWEET BAY

The evergreen bay is closely linked to Italian Renaissance gardens where it makes hedges and green architectural shapes, such as *exedrae*. With spicy aromatic foliage, this somewhat tender, large shrub or tree is commonly grown as a potted specimen at the centre of herb gardens. Paired standards can also be used to frame a door.

Cultivation Well-drained fertile soil, in full sun. Good in mild seaside gardens where it can reach substantial proportions. Use secateurs (pruners) to avoid unsightly, half-cut leaves, and prune in the summer. In cold areas, stand pot-grown standards and spirals in a conservatory over winter, move to a sheltered corner next to the house or insulate *in situ*.

Varieties *Laurus nobilis* has a number of varieties, but the species is the main topiary plant. (Frost hardy/Z 8–10)

Uses Lollipop-headed standards as well as spirals, cones, obelisks and hedges.

Problems Susceptible to scale insect, the first sign of which is often sooty mould on the leaves. Beware leaf scorch and frost damage in hard winters.

Lavandula

LAVENDER

A deliciously aromatic herb, it was once a popular knot-garden plant. Also a favourite for path edging in cottage gardens, lavender not only smells wonderful but is a terrific bee magnet. Even after flowering, the narrow greyish green or silver evergreen foliage keeps plants looking good all year round.

Cultivation Prefers sharply drained alkaline ground; avoid soil that remains wet in winter because it causes plants to rot and makes them much more susceptible to the cold. Clip over immediately after flowering, or in mid-spring before new growth occurs, to encourage a dense, bushy habit. Remove spent flower stems plus the shoot tips, but do not cut into old wood.

Varieties Forms of *Lavandula angustifolia* are compact and ideal for clipping, and come in a range of soft pastel flower colours, such as 'Loddon Pink'. For knots and low edging choose dwarf forms, such as *L. a.* 'Munstead' or the dark-purple flowering 'Hidcote'. (Hardy/Z 6–9)

Uses Low hedges; knots and domes; informal dwarf standards for pots.

Problems Hard winters can be lethal. Unless clipped annually, plants become open and threadbare. Take care when pruning as branches are brittle. May die if cut hard back.

Ligustrum

PRIVET

Common privet (*Ligustrum vulgare*) has long been popular for everyday topiary with a menagerie of animals

and birds emerging from the tops of hedges in cottage and suburban gardens. The glossy foliage will survive in all but the harshest winters, and, with frequent clipping, the leaves get smaller and the branching more dense, allowing for shapes with fine detail.

L. delavayanum has recently become popular, its tiny leaves and pliable stems making it a good substitute for the slower-growing box in topiary frames.

Cultivation Fertile, reasonably well-drained, humus-rich soil, preferably in full sun, but will tolerate shade. Mulching with well-rotted stable manure aids growth as privet is notoriously greedy. Clip established hedges in late spring and early autumn or midsummer only, but clip topiary animals and other figures frequently during summer to keep them in shape.

Varieties *L. vulgare* (semi-evergreen which is suitable for hedging and topiary; hardy/Z 5–9); *L. ovalifolium* (hardy/Z 6–10) is similar with a number of colourful variegated forms, like gold-splashed *L. o.* 'Aureum'; *L. delavayanum* (tiny dark-leaved evergreen suitable for fine detail clipping and training over wire formers; hardy/Z 8–10).

Uses Hedging, arches and other architectural features, birds and animals. The small-leaved *L. delavayanum* is often grown as a round-headed standard.

Problems Semi-evergreen types may lose their foliage in cold winters. *L. delavayanum* needs protection in cold areas.

Laburnum × *watereri* 'Vossii'

Laurus nobilis

Lavandula angustifolia 'Hidcote'

Lonicera nitida 'Baggesen's Gold'

Lonicera nitida
HONEYSUCKLE

The shrubby *Lonicera nitida* is ideal for impatient topiarists because it not only looks like box but grows much more quickly. Its drawback is that it needs more frequent clipping, and large figures may eventually become threadbare and wobbly.

Cultivation Grows on most soils in sun or, especially in the case of 'Baggesen's Gold', light shade, and is quite hardy. Tolerates salt spray. Having flexible stems, designs can be quite complex, but large pieces are best trained over a wire frame for extra stability. Trim two or three times a year, as necessary, to maintain a neat form.

Varieties *L. n.* 'Baggesen's Gold' has gold-variegated leaves. (Hardy/Z 7–9)

Uses For medium, round-topped hedges, simple geometric sculptures, such as balls and domes, as well as animal and bird figures, perhaps trained over wire.

Problems 'Baggesen's Gold' often reverts to all-green shoots which should be cut out at source as soon as possible. It can be scorched by strong sun on dry ground and harsh winters may defoliate the stems.

Myrtus
MYRTLE

Although it is not completely hardy, this glossy, evergreen, aromatic shrub is nevertheless still much sought after as a topiary plant. The small, dark green leaves are broad with an elegant point and, in summer, the dense, bushy stems are covered in tiny, white fragrant blooms that open from spherical buds.

Cultivation Best grown in containers so that plants can be moved to an unheated conservatory over winter. When grown in the ground, choose a warm, sheltered, well-drained spot on fertile soil. Clip in summer.

Varieties *Myrtus communis* and the cream-edged 'Microphylla Variegata'. (Frost hardy/Z 9–10)

Uses Balls, domes and small standards.

Problems Being slightly tender, winter protection is vital to avoid the cold and wet.

Osmanthus
FALSE OR SWEET HOLLY

Osmanthus has several tonsile forms (i.e. suitable for clipping) which, with their sweetly fragrant blooms, are ideal for the cottage or courtyard garden. The stems of the box look-alikes, *O. delavayi* and *O. × burkwoodii*, are also flexible, making it possible to train them over a frame.

Cultivation Grows on most soils including clay, and tolerates full sun or partial shade. Clip immediately after flowering, and as necessary during the summer.

Varieties *O. delavayi* and *O. × burkwoodii* both have small, dark green leaves and tiny, white spring blossoms. *O. heterophyllus* looks like holly and has attractive, variegated forms. (Frost hardy/Z 7–9)

Uses Hedging, standards, domes, mushrooms and for growing over topiary frames.

Problems Few, though some types need clipping regularly to avoid becoming shaggy.

Phillyrea

This hardy, historic topiary plant, which had its heyday in the 17th century, is now quite difficult to find. The dark, leathery, green leaves, paler on the reverse side, clip to form a dense, even surface, ideal for large architectural features.

Cultivation Easy on any reasonable soil, in sun or shade; salt tolerant. Clip or prune in spring and in late summer.

Varieties *Phillyrea angustifolia* is the best for topiary. (Hardy/Z 7–9)

Uses Geometric forms, green architecture and formal hedging.

Problems Limited availability.

Pinus
PINE

One of the principal plants for cloud pruning, pine has several species and cultivars which can be trained. Some have the desired aged look with gnarled, twisted branches and, with additional training, such as wiring, can be shaped to form elegant tufts of pine needles on bare, curving stems.

Cultivation Pines are usually very tough and easy to grow on a range of soils. Japanese black pine (*Pinus thunbergii*) is drought tolerant and can even be grown on sand. The new growth occurs in pale coloured "candles". To shape the tree, remove the top half of the candles in spring to encourage side branching. Keep the ones you need and snip off the rest. Bamboo canes and wire can be used to train pines into more characterful shapes.

Varieties *P. thunbergii* (hardy/Z 5–8) for large, cloud-pruned trees in the ground or, for controlling the size, in containers; *P. sylvestris* 'Watereri' (for multi-stemmed, spreading cloud topiaries in large containers; hardy/Z 3–7); *P. mugo* (dwarf cultivars; hardy/Z 3–7) for domes and small, potted cloud topiaries.

Uses Cloud topiary; low hummocks.

Problems Soft young shoots may be attacked by caterpillars.

Pittosporum

The New Zealand kohuhu (*Pittosporum tenuifolium*) has light green, wavy-edged leaves borne on black stems, making it popular with flower arrangers. Although the tiny blooms are insignificant, most are fragrant. Variegated and coloured leaf forms are available, but they are less hardy than the species.

Cultivation Salt tolerant and ideal for mild seaside or city gardens, it grows in any well-drained soil including ones containing lime. The species prefers some shade. Variegated and purple plants make good container subjects for large patio tubs. Trim to shape in late spring or midsummer. In colder gardens protect the roots from frost using a deep bark mulch.

Varieties 'Abbotsbury Gold' (gold marbling) and 'Silver Queen' (white variegation) are two of the best cultivars. The latter is relatively hardy and has a naturally compact, pyramidal habit. (Frost hardy/Z 9–10)

Myrtus communis

Osmanthus delavayi

Pinus mugo

Pittosporum tenuifolium cultivar

Uses *P. tenuifolium* can be used for hedging in mild seaside gardens, otherwise trim to simple dome or cone shapes.

Problems May be killed by frost in cold winters.

Prunus
LAUREL

The cherry laurel (*Prunus laurocerasus*) is a glossy, large-leaved plant, mainly used for hedging. The Portugal laurel (*P. lusitanica*) has smaller, pointed leaves on contrasting red stems, and is more versatile for topiary and a good substitute for the tender bay tree which is prone to cold, wet winters.

Cultivation Tolerates any soil, including clay, provided it is not waterlogged in the winter. Cherry laurel dislikes thin chalky soils, but the Portugal laurel is relatively lime tolerant. To avoid unsightly half-cut leaves, it is best to trim with secateurs (pruners).

Varieties *P. laurocerasus* 'Rotundifolia' is good for creating formal hedging; the white-marbled 'Castlewellan' is less vigorous with a narrower leaf. *P. lusitanica* 'Myrtifolia' (and the variegated *P. l.* 'Variegata' are slower growing. (Frost hardy/Z 7–9)

Uses Ideal for creating quick-growing hedges and screens. Older specimens of cherry laurel can be converted into large dome or mushroom-headed standards. For tall, robust, round or dome-headed standards choose *P. lusitanica* or *P. l.* 'Myrtifolia'.

Problems Relatively trouble free.

Pyracantha
FIRETHORN

Grown for its small, pointed, glossy foliage, creamy white blossom and heavy crops of ornamental berries, firethorn can also be clipped and trained to cover a house wall.

Cultivation Hardy firethorn tolerates a wide range of soils, including clay, but is unhappy on thin, chalky soils; will cover north- and east-facing walls. Train on wires to form a network of horizontal branches. For improved berry displays, once the embryonic fruits start to develop in summer, cut back lateral shoots to expose them. Prune again in spring to remove some old flowering wood and to make room for new growth.

Varieties The gold-fruited 'Golden Charmer' and orange-red 'Orange Glow' are two of the best for berries and most resistant to disease (both hardy/Z 6–9); 'Teton' (red; hardy/Z 5) is also good, although susceptible to fireblight which can transfer from hawthorn hedging.

Uses Espalier-style coverage of walls; wall-trained columns and clipped door surrounds.

Problems Many varieties are prone to scab which affects fruiting. Check labels to ensure you pick scab-resistant cultivars like 'Orange Glow'. Birds eat all colours of berry. Hard pruning may sacrifice fruits.

Quercus ilex
HOLM OAK

Quite unlike deciduous oaks and looking more like holly, hence the species name, this evergreen is a useful plant for producing hedges and screens as well as large geometric shapes.

Cultivation Needs deep, well-drained soil and full sun. Use only young plants or there may be problems getting established. Grows particularly well in mild coastal gardens although it is hardy. Clip in late summer.

Varieties *Quercus ilex* is the only suitable topiary species. (Frost hardy/Z 7–9)

Uses Hedging and green architectural shapes, especially large cylinders.

Problems Healthy, robust specimens have good natural resistance.

Rhamnus alaternus
ITALIAN BUCKTHORN

Like *Phillyrea*, the Italian buckthorn was once a popular topiary and hedging plant in the 17th century. Now the plain green species is rarely used, being superseded by the showy, cream-variegated 'Argenteovariegata'.

Cultivation Though frost hardy, the variegated form does best in mild regions or sheltered gardens, and makes a fine wall-covering for even shady sites. Any reasonable, well-drained soil.

Varieties *Rhamnus alaternus* 'Argenteovariegata' has cream-edged leaves. (Frost hardy/Z 7–9)

Uses Large domes, broad round-topped cones and for a formal, clipped wall-covering trained on wires.

Problems Relatively trouble free.

Rosmarinus
ROSEMARY

It is hard to believe that such an undisciplined shrub could ever have been trained into fanciful shapes, but, along with juniper, this aromatic herb was once widely used in topiary. Wiry stems are covered in tufts of narrow, dark green leaves and, in early spring, the species produces an abundance of pale grey-blue flowers.

Cultivation Grow on sharply drained soil or in containers, in full sun. Provide a sheltered spot in cold regions, such as against a warm wall.

Varieties *Rosmarinus officinalis* and *R. o.* 'Miss Jessopp's Upright' are the hardiest and most useful, the latter especially for hedging. (Frost hardy/Z 7–9)

Uses Medium-sized hedges, especially in mild gardens; small standards; simple geometric shapes (trained over wire frames).

Problems Brittle stems may break off during training. Vulnerable to frost.

Taxus
YEW

A superlative topiary plant and one of the best materials for producing sharp-edged, green architecture and crisp, geometric forms. The gold-leaved cultivars make a pleasing contrast against dark green, and glow in shade or on dull days. Irish yew (*Taxus baccata* 'Fastigiata') requires little training and is useful for marking entrances, creating avenues or when planted alone as an exclamation mark. Yew is poisonous to livestock.

Quercus ilex

Rhamnus alaternus 'Argenteovariegata'

Rosmarinus officinalis

Rosmarinus officinalis

Taxus (gold-leaved cultivar)

Cultivation Grows on a range of soils provided they are well drained; drought tolerant once established. Sun or shade. Best planted in mild winter periods but, if planting in early summer, water thoroughly every two weeks during dry spells to aid establishment. Clip hedges and geometric shapes annually, ideally during the latter half of summer or, for really fine topiary, in the first half of summer and then again in early autumn. More complex figures can be trained through wire or on metal frames. Irish yew produces multiple leading shoots which should be cut back when they start to elongate. This prevents the stems from splaying out and negates the need for wiring. Do not use yew for long-term container growth.

Varieties *T. baccata* (hardy/Z 6–7) has many forms and several gold-leaved cultivars, such as *T. b.* 'Elegantissima' (a golden yew with a broadly upright habit); *T. b.* 'Fastigiata' (narrow columnar habit); *T. b.* Fastigiata Aurea Group (gold form of species); *T.* x *media* cultivars (cross between Japanese and English yew; hardy/Z 5–7) and grown in the United States in place of *T. baccata*. A drought-tolerant plant for hedging or green architecture.

Uses Formal hedging (including green architecture, such as buttresses and finials); geometric shapes, such as cones, pyramids, domes and obelisks. Yew houses and mushroom-headed standards; tunnels; organic, free-flowing hedging; abstract sculptures and figurative shapes.

Problems Avoid poorly drained soils as susceptible to phytophthora root rot. Not good in containers.

Thuja
ARBORVITAE

This aromatic conifer has long been used for creating formal hedges and green architectural shapes and produces a fine, even surface when clipped. Western red cedar (*Thuja plicata*) has rich green foliage which makes a good contrast with dark evergreen yew and holly.

Cultivation Best on deep, moisture-retentive soil. Wind tolerant once established, but shelter when young using windbreak mesh. Clip once in late spring or, for extra control, again towards the end of summer. Do not cut back the leading shoot until the plant reaches its desired height.

Varieties *T. occidentalis* (white cedar; hardy/Z 3–8) and its forms, and *T. plicata* (western red cedar; hardy/Z 6–8) and its forms.

Uses Large hedges, screens and green architectural shapes, such as colonnades, arches and *exedrae*.

Problems Generally trouble free.

Tilia
LIME, LINDEN

The soft pliable stems and quick growth rate of these hardy deciduous trees make them the perfect choice for pollarded screens which take up far less room than traditional hedges, and also allow more light through. In winter, the skeletal structure is a bonus. Lime has large, pale or dark green, heart-shaped leaves and small fragrant flowers in summer. Though the common lime (*Tilia* x *europaea*) has a reputation for dropping sticky honeydew, other forms are safer. Flowers of *T.* x *euchlora* often intoxicate bees.

Cultivation Rich, deep, moisture-retentive soils are best. Prune during the dormant period, removing all growth not needed for training and which grows out from the horizontal supports. Remove suckers from the base of *T.* x *europaea*.

Varieties *T.* x *europaea* has now largely been superseded by *T.* x *euchlora* because it is resistant to aphids and doesn't produce suckers. Large-leaved lime (*T. platyphyllos* 'Rubra') has red winter shoots. (Hardy/Z 4–7)

Uses Pleached screens, formal avenues and covered walkways.

Problems Depending on the form used, aphids and suckering.

Tsuga
HEMLOCK

Western hemlock (*Tsuga heterophylla*) is a hedging conifer that, like yew, will regrow if cut back hard. It is well suited to warm maritime regions with a high rainfall.

Cultivation Western hemlock thrives on moist, neutral to acid soils. Protect from cold drying winds, especially when getting established. If the soil is limey, and the site exposed, try eastern hemlock (*T. canadensis*) instead. Pinch out the growing shoots to encourage dense, bushy growth, and clip twice in the main summer growing period once the desired shape has been reached.

Varieties Eastern hemlock (*T. canadensis*; hardy/Z 3) and western hemlock (*T. heterophylla*; hardy/Z 6–8).

Uses Hedges and simple green architectural shapes.

Problems Suffers in polluted city locations and won't tolerate drought.

Viburnum tinus
LAURUSTINUS

This evergreen is a tough species with medium-sized, dark green oval leaves. From autumn to spring the plants produce a succession of white, honey-scented flower clusters and, when several plants are grown together, good crops of dark metallic-blue berries may follow.

Cultivation Tolerates any reasonable soil, from clay to thin chalk, and is happy in shade. Trim for shape after flowering, in spring. Standards may be trained from seedlings, but use rooted cuttings from a good clone for the best flowering performance.

Varieties 'Eve Price' (compact and free-flowering), 'Gwenllian' (pink-tinged flowers and buds, less vigorous than the species), and the tender, cream-splashed 'Variegatum'. (Frost hardy/Z 7–9)

Uses Flowering standards, broad cones, wall-trained half cones.

Problems Generally trouble free, but sooty mould on leaves may indicate scale insects, aphids or white-fly. Spray with systemic insecticide.

Taxus baccata

Thuja plicata 'Irish Gold'

Tilia

Viburnum tinus 'Eve Price'

glossary

Alleé French term for an avenue or a long, straight walkway in a garden, usually leading to a vista or focal point.

Batter The word used to describe the sloping face of a formal hedge that has been cut to receive even light from top to bottom.

Berceau A pergola walkway that may be covered with decorative *treillage* panels or clipped walls of plants like hornbeam.

Buttress Originally describing the sloping brick or carved stone supports used to strengthen walls at regular intervals, the word is also used with regard to formal hedging. This can be made to look more like green masonry and develop character and weight by the addition of similarly shaped extensions.

Cake stand A topiary shape consisting of a series of circular disks or sections stacked on top of one another with short gaps in between them.

Chlorophyll A term used to describe moss-filled topiary frames planted with ivies and other surface-rooting plants.

Clairvoyée French term for window-like apertures cut into hedges, screens or into a *berceau*.

Cloud pruning Topiary technique from the Far East which creates stylized trees with cloud-like formations of clipped greenery at the tips of bare stems.

Colonnade A series of connected, classically styled archways clipped from hedging.

Crocks Traditionally collected from broken terracotta pots, crocks are used to cover the drainage holes in containers to prevent them clogging up with potting mix.

Dibber A narrow, blunt-ended tool used for making planting holes, such as in the compacted sphagnum moss used to fill topiary frames.

Espalier A type of wall training for top fruit and woody ornamentals that consists of horizontal branches coming off a central stem.

Exedra A semi-circular wall or hedge that often accommodates a curved bench seat or circular paving feature, perhaps at the end of a vista or pathway.

Finial A flourish atop a gatepost or pillar or, in topiary terms, decorative elements along the top of formal hedging, or to decorate the top of a topiary piece or green pillar.

Frame An open structure of trellis, metal mesh or wire used to train plants to a particular shape. A frame can be put over a plant, which is then clipped when it grows through the mesh, and it could also be used to tie branches onto it, or, in the case of ivy, to weave stems through. Moss-filled frames are used for instant effect and are referred to as "chlorophyll".

Humus A substance, such as garden compost or well-rotted horse manure, that is applied to soil to make it more friable and moisture retentive.

Knot An interconnecting pattern of low hedging which was popular in Elizabethan times.

Labyrinth A maze-like pattern, often marked out into the turf, which presents the walker with a complex and narrow pathway. The journey through the labyrinth and the design itself has, for some, a spiritual or religious symbolism.

Leader The principal shoot or central stem of a plant.

Leg The long, unbranched stem supporting the head of a standard.

Maze A complex pattern, usually of tall formal hedging to prevent cheating, that can lead the walker down blind alleys and away from the target. The goal in this game or puzzle is reaching the centre.

Mulch The word has several definitions and may include a material such as chipped bark that is applied thickly onto the ground to help prevent weeds and keep the soil moist or to some kind of decorative aggregate used principally to colour the ground in parterres and knots. Both may be used on top of a black landscaping fabric which acts as a semi-permeable membrane.

Niche A shallow door- or window-shaped indent cut into a hedge. This may accommodate a statue or urn on a plinth.

Obelisk A tapering geometric figure with a square profile that may be topped with a pyramid or ball-shaped finial. In topiary, frames are often used to achieve this crisp, well-proportioned shape.

Parterre A simple or complex pattern created from low, clipped hedging. It differs from the knot in that the sections are not interconnected.

Parterre de broderie A type of elaborate parterre pattern that resembles embroidered flowers, leaves and tendrils.

Pinch out Remove the shoot tip with thumb and forefinger (usually this is a bud and a few developing leaves). Pinching out causes the stem to produce multiple side branches and this technique is used in the formation of ball-headed or flowering standards, as well as to make thinly branched topiary specimens thicken up.

Pleaching The horizontal training of branches along wires to create open screens. The stems may be grafted together in order to form continuous lines.

Plug A small, rooted cutting or seedling that has been grown in a cellular tray, thereby forming the roots into a narrow wedge shape that is ideal for planting up chlorophyll topiaries.

Plumb line A piece of string with a weight suspended from the end which acts as a guide for checking that lines are perfectly vertical.

Standard A type of topiary with a long clean "leg" topped with a round, domed, weeping or other geometrically shaped head. Figurative forms like birds may also be grown on a leg.

Stilt hedge A formal hedge which is allowed to develop only after the individual stems or stilts have reached a certain height, usually above your head.

Swag Loops usually made from rope twisted round with ivy trails that connect a series of uprights or decorate a window trough.

Treillage A term derived from the French, this word refers to ornately shaped pieces of trellis.

gardens to visit

The following is by no means a comprehensive list but it does include some of the finest topiary and formal gardens that are open to the public in Europe and the United States. It is wise to check opening times to avoid disappointment using a good garden guidebook or Internet listings. There are many superb private topiary gardens and some of these open their gates on occasional days or by appointment. Topiary is, of course, found worldwide. Cloud- pruned trees, for example, decorate the gardens of many a temple, monastery or private residence in the East.

BRITISH ISLES

Arley Hall, Arley, Northwich, Cheshire

Athelhampton, Athelhampton, Dorchester, Dorset

Barnsley House, Barnsley, Cirencester, Gloucestershire

Belton House, Grantham, Lincolnshire

Biddulph Grange, Stoke-on-Trent, Staffordshire

Blickling Hall, Blickling, Aylsham, Norfolk

Bodrhyddan, Rhuddlan, Denbighshire, Wales

Brickwall House, Northiam, Rye, East Sussex

Chatsworth House, Bakewell, Derbyshire

Chenies Manor, Chenies, Buckinghamshire

Chirk Castle, Chirk, Nr Wrexham, North Wales

Clipsham Yew Walk, Clipsham, Rutland

Cliveden, Taplow, Buckinghamshire

Cranbourne Manor Garden, Wimborne, Dorset

Doddington Hall, Lincoln, Lincolnshire

Dorney Court, Dorney, Windsor, Berkshire

Drummond Castle, Muthill, Crieff, Tayside, Scotland

Elsing Hall, Elsing, Nr Dereham, Norfolk

Elvaston Castle, Elvaston, Derbyshire

Piet Bekaert's Garden, Belgium

Erddig, Wrexham, North Wales

Ham House, Ham, Richmond, Surrey

Hampton Court Palace, Hampton Wick, East Molesey, Surrey

Harewood House, Leeds, Yorkshire

Hatfield House, Hatfield, Hertfordshire

Helmingham Hall, Stowmarket, Suffolk

Hever Castle, Edenbridge, Kent

Hidcote Manor, Chipping Camden, Gloucestershire

Knightshayes, Tiverton, Devon

Lamport Hall, Northampton, Northamptonshire

Leeds Castle, Maidstone, Kent

Levens Hall, Kendal, Cumbria

Longleat House, Warminster, Wiltshire

Mapperton House, Beaminster, Dorset

Megginch Castle, Errol, Perthshire, Nr Perth, Tayside, Scotland

Melbourne Hall, Melbourne, Derbyshire

Mitton Manor, Penkridge, Staffordshire

Mount Stewart, Co. Down, Northern Ireland

Parnham House, Parnham, Beaminster, Dorset

Peover Hall, Over Peover, Knutsford, Cheshire

Pitmedden, Udney, Ellon, Aberdeenshire, Scotland

Plas Brondanw, Gwynedd, Wales

Powis Castle, Powys, Wales

Renishaw Hall, Renishaw, Derbyshire

Rodmarton Manor, Cirencester, Gloucestershire

Rousham House, Bicester Oxfordshire

Sudeley Castle, Winchcombe, Gloucestershire

RHS Chelsea Flower Show

RHS Chelsea Flower Show

Rousham House, Oxfordshire

Chenies Manor, Oxfordshire

Tatton Hall Gardens, Knutsford, Cheshire

Trentham Gardens, Stoke on Trent, Staffordshire

Walmer Castle, Walmer, Deal, Kent

West Green House, Hartley Wintney, Basingstoke, Hampshire

Wollerton Old Hall, Wollerton, Market Drayton, Shropshire

Wyken Hall, Bury St Edmunds, Suffolk

FRANCE

Château d'Angers, Loire Valley

Château de Breteuil, Yvelines

Château du Pin, Fabras, Ardeche

Chenonceaux, Indre-et-Loire

Courances, Essonne

Eyrignac, Salignac, Dordogne

Le Parc Oriental, Loire Valley

Vaux-le-Vicomte, Seine-et-Marne

Versailles, Yvelines

Villandry, Indre-et-Loire

GERMANY AND AUSTRIA

Herrenhausen, Hanover, Lower Saxony, Germany

Schönbrunn, Vienna, Austria

Schwetzingen, Baden-Württemberg, Germany

Veitshöchheim, Bavaria, Germany

ITALY

Castello Balduino, Montalto (Pavia) Lombardy

Giardino Giusti, Verona, Veneto

Isola Bella, Lazo Maggiore (Novara) Lombardy

Palazzo Farnese, Caprarola, near Viterbo

Villa Allegri Arvedi, V. Cuzzoni, Veneto

Villa Gamberaia, Settignano (Florence), Tuscany

Villa Garzoni, Collodi (Lucca), Tuscany

Villa La Pietra, Florence, Tuscany

Villa Lante della Rovere, Bagnaria (Viterbo) Lazio

Villa Marlia, Lucca, Tuscany

Villa Pisani, Strà, Veneto

Villa Rizzardi, Pojega di Negrar (Verona) Veneto

LOW COUNTRIES

Château de Beloeil, Nr Mons, Belgium

Het Loo, Apeldoorn, Gelderland, The Netherlands

Huis Bingerden, Ligging, Angerio, The Netherlands

Kasteel Twickel, Delden, The Netherlands

Middachten, De Steeg, Gelderland, The Netherlands

Parc des Topiares, Durbuy, Prov. de Liège, Belgium

Weldam Castle, Goor, The Netherlands

UNITED STATES

Colonial Williamsburg, Williamsburg, Virginia

Filoli Historic House and Gardens, Woodside, California

Green Animals, Portsmouth, Rhode Island

Ladew Topiary Gardens, Monkton, Maryland

Longwood Gardens, Kennett Square, Pennsylvania

Mount Vernon, Mount Vernon, Virginia

Nemours Mansion and Gardens, Wilmington, Delaware

Walt Disney World, Lake Buena Vista, Florida

Lamport Hall, Northampton, Northamptonshire

Peover Hall, Knutsford, Cheshire

suppliers and organisations

EUROPE

Agrumi Ltd
Sway Road
Lymington SO41 6FR
Tel: 01590 683487
www.agrumi.co.uk
Wholesale nursery
www.topiaryart,co.uk
Bespoke topiary plant sculptures

**EBTS: The European Boxwood
and Topiary Society**
www.ebts.org
*Topiary society, with offices in the UK, France,
Germany, the Netherlands, Belgium and USA*

Bellamont Topiary
Long Bredy
Dorchester DT2 9HN
Tel: 01308 482247
www.bellamont-topiary.co.uk
Topiary plants

The Classic Gardener Nursery
Pound Barn, West Kington
Chippenham, Wiltshire
SN14 7JQ
Tel: 01249 783880
www.classicgardener.co.uk
Topiary plants

Crown Topiary
234 North Road
Hertford SG14 2PW
Tel: 01992 501055
www.crowntopiary.co.uk
Topiary plants

Earlstone Box and Topiary
Earlstone Manor Farm
Burghclere, Newbury
Berkshire RG20 9NG
Tel: 01635 278648
www.earlstoneboxandtopiary.co.uk
Topiary plants

Folia Europe
Well End Road,
Borehamwood
Hertfordshire WD6 5NZ
Tel: 020 8953 5827
www.folia-europe.com
Topiary and hedging plants

Grasslands Nursery
Free Green Lane
Peover, Knutsford, WA16 9QY
Tel: 01565 723831
www.grasslands.co.uk
Topiary and hedging plants

Hedges Direct
Tel: 01257 263873
www.hedgesdirect.co.uk
Online nursery for all kinds of hedging

Highfield Hollies
Highfield Farm, Hatch Lane, Liss,
Hampshire GU33 7NH
Tel: 01730 892372
(visits by appointment only)
www.highfieldhollies.com
*Holly and holly topiary, including the National
Collection of hollies*

King & Co
Pods Lane, Rayne
Braintree, Essex CM77 6WF
Tel: 01376 340469
www.kingco.co.uk
Tree and hedging plants nursery

Orchard Nurseries
1 The Laurels
Whitley, DN14 0GZ
Tel: 01977 663073
www.orchardnurseries.co.uk
Topiary plants

Paramount Plants and Gardens
131 Theobalds Park Road
Enfield, London EN2 9BH
Tel: 020 8367 8809
www.paramountplants.co.uk
Topiary plants

Prestige Plants
Blacksmiths Lane
Stowmarket, Suffolk IP14
Tel: 07929 170366
e-mail: enquiries@prestigeplants.co.uk
www.prestigeplants.co.uk

River Garden Nurseries
Troutbeck, Otford,
Sevenoaks, Kent TN14 5PH
Tel: 01959 525588; Mob: 07717 277175
e-mail: box@river-garden.co.uk
www.river-garden.co.uk
Box and box topiary

The Romantic Garden Nursery
The Street, Norwich
Norfolk NR9 5NW
tel: 01603 261488
www.romantic-garden-nursery.co.uk
Topiary plants

Seagrave Nurseries
84 Melton Road
Barrow Upon Soar, LE12 8NX
Tel: 01509 621300
www.seagravenurseries.co.uk
Topiary plants

Top Topiary
Tel: 01590 730075
www.toptopiary.co.uk
Online nursery including topiary frames

Topiary Art Designs Ltd
Millers Meadow, Grimstone End
Bury-St-Edmunds, Suffolk IP31 2LZ
Tel: 01359 232303
e-mail: steve@topiaryartdesigns.com
www.topiaryartdesigns.com
Topiary frames

Topiary Frames by Brian Joyce
9 Ash Grove
Wheathampstead AL4 8DF
Tel: 01582 629724
email: admin@wheathampstead.net
www.wheathampstead.net/topiary
Topiary frames made to order

Topiary Hire
Unit 34, 67-68 Hatton Garden
London , EC1 8JY
Tel: 020 7125 0215
e-mail: info@topiary-hire.co.uk
www.topiaryhire.co.uk
Topiary plants for hire for events

NORTH AMERICA
The American Boxwood Society
www.boxwoodsociety.org
e-mail: info@boxwoodsociety.org
Topiary society

Chris' Topiary Nursery
9004 Copley Lane
Riverside, CA 92503
Tel: 951 352 3526
e-mail: mrtopiary@charter.net
webpages.charter.net/mrtopiary
Topiary plants and bespoke frames

Cliff Finch's Zoo
16923 North Friant Road
Friant, California 93626
Tel: 559 822 2315
e-mail: info@topiaryzoo.com
www.topiaryzoo.com
Ivy and traditional topiary, plus frames

Greenpiece Wire Art
PO Box 260, Bridge Station
Niagara Falls
New York 14305
Tel: 800 246 6984
e-mail: info@braungroup.com
www.greenpiecewireart.com
Topiary frames

Hickory Hollow Nursery
713 Route 17
Tuxedo, NY 10987
Tel: 845 351 7226
email: hickoryhollow@optonline.net
www.hickoryhollownursery.com
Topiary plants

Meadowbrook Farm
1633 Washington Lane
Jenkintown, PA 19046
Tel: 215 887 5900

e-mail: phs-info@pennhort.org
meadowbrookfarm.org
Topiary frames and moss-filled forms by mail order

Noah's Ark Topiary
Tel: 727 300 1877
www.noahsarktopiary.com
Online topiary frames

Old Garden Topiary
3923 Victoria Avenue
Nanaimo, BC V9T 2A1, Canada
Tel: 250 729 0211
www.oldgardentopiary.com
Topiary plants and frames

AUSTRALIA
Garden Express
470 Monbulk Road
Monbulk, Victoria 3793
Tel: 1300 606 242
www.gardenexpress.com.au
Online topiary plants

Misty Downs Nursery
Tel: 0418 599 229
www.thegardentrough.com.au
Online topiary shrubs and plants

Totally Topiary
Tel: 0410 404 422
email: totallytopiary@gmail.com
www.totallytopiary.com.au
Supplier of topiary plants

NEW ZEALAND
Standards of Excellence
Main road RD2
Katikati, New Zealand
Tel: 07 549 0852
www.topiary plants.co.nz
Online topiary shrubs and plants, nursery open by appointment

index

Author's acknowledgements

Special thanks are due to my friends and associates in the European Boxwood and Topiary Society, many of whom have contributed to the background research. I would also like to give a big thank you to Jenny Alban-Davies of River Garden Nurseries, Steve Manning of Topiary Art Designs, Judy Older and The Topiary Shop for providing materials and facilities, and for demonstrating the practical step-by-step sequences. In addition I'm very grateful to garden designer Fiona Henley and professional topiarist Simon Rose for helping to source some unique photographic locations and, of course, to Steve Wooster whose images are an inspiration. And, finally, thanks to all the designers, topiarists and gardeners worldwide whose creations have been brought together for others to appreciate within the pages of this book.

Publisher's acknowledgements

The publisher would like to thank the following garden owners, designers and institutions for allowing their gardens to be photographed for the purposes of this book. All photographs in this book were taken by Steven Wooster, unless otherwise stated.

t = top b = bottom c = centre l = left r = right
Arley Hall, Cheshire 8tl; 49b; 51t; 72; 79b; 103b; 106; 107t; 158r
Athelhampton House and Gardens, Dorset 34–35; 49t; 50t; 61; 69r; 86; 88bl
Bosvigo House, Truro, Cornwall 27; 105t
Chateau d'Angers 57tr; 128l
Chateau du Pin 2-3; 45t; 60tl; 64; 65tr; 71b; 83tl; 100; 116–117; 159tl; 160r
Chaumont Flower Festival, France 2001 129; 133l
Chenies Manor, Buckinghamshire 5bl; 17; 36; 41b; 75; 79tl; 119; 120; 153; 155tr
East Ruston Old Vicarage, Norwich 59b; 99 (photographer Jo Whitworth)
Ellerslee Flower Show, New Zealand 2003 24t
Elsing Hall, Norfolk 5bl; 43t; 48br; 87; 101b; 160l
Elvaston Castle back cover right; 6; 47t; 51b; 53b; 107bl; 107br; 156r
Grahame Dawson & Alex Ross, Auckland, New Zealand 74
The Garden in Mind, Hampshire 82t; 130 (cloud topiary steps; photographer: Jo Whitworth) (designer: Ivan Hicks)
Fiona Henley Design, Hampshire back cover middle; 7; 12–13; 14; 27tr; 41t; 53tl;

53tr; 104b; 105b; 159bl
Iford Manor, Bradford-Upon-Avon, Wiltshire 26 (photographer: Jo Whitworth)
Mr. and Mrs. John Lewis, Shute House, Dorset (photographer Sarah Cuttle)
John Tordoff, London (owner and designer) 137t
Judy Older, Kent 22t; 23b; 40b; 82bl; 83bl; 93tl; 122l
't Kragenhof, Belgium 19t; 28; 55; 62l
Kristina Fitzsimmons, London 56
Lamport Hall, Nottinghamshire 155bl (photographer: Peter Anderson)
Leeann Roots (owner and designer) 8br
Mapperton Gardens, Dorset 19b; 40t; 45b; 80b
Parc Oriental, France 25t; 131t; 131bl; 134; 142; 156l; 159tr
Peover Hall, Cheshire 81t; 103t; 155br
Piet Bekaert's Garden, Belgium front cover, 4br; 10 (both); 29tr; 29b; 47b; 85br; 102r; 109; 128r; 135; 154t
Renishaw Hall, Sheffield 18t; 38l; 42b; 43b; 79tr; 144l; 144r; 145r; 158l
RHS Chelsea Flower Show 1999 29tl; 154br ("Sculpture in the Garden", designer: George Carter) (photographer: Jonathan Buckley)
RHS Chelsea Flower Show 2000 68 (photographer Jonathan Buckley)
RHS Chelsea Flower Show 2003 5cr (top); 8bl (Help the Aged Garden); 27tl (The Romantic Garden Nursery); cover spine; 108l; 108r (Topiary Arts Garden); 111 (Topiary Arts Garden); 112r (The Romantic Garden Nursery); 113bl (Topiary Arts Garden); 131r; 154bl (Topiary Arts Garden); 159br
RHS Tatton Park Flower Show 2002 31tl ("Garden of Illusion", designers: Andy Stockton, Daniel Sterry and Marylynn Abbott)
Rodmarton Manor 16l; 21bl; 76l; 78l; 84; 89b; 145l
Rousham House, Oxfordshire 155tl
Simon Rose 23t; 48bl
Sir Miles Warren, Christchurch, New Zealand 157r
Tofuku-ji Temple, Kyoto, Japan 54tl
Steve Manning, Bury-St-Edmunds 66r; 89t; 118; 121; 122r; 123t; 123b;136r
Villandry, France 1, 5cl (top); 9t; 52; 57tl; 57b; 58; 60tr; 65tl; 88br; 90l; 90r; 91; 93b; 101tc; 157l
West Green House, near Hartney Witney, Hampshire (owner and designer: Marylynn Abbott) 5c bottom; 59tr (photographer Jo Whitworth);
Wollerton Old Hall, Shropshire 16tr; 21t; 22b; 43br; 46l; 46r; 70l; 98r; 102l; 104t
Wyken Hall, Suffolk back cover left; 20b;

37; 38r; 76r; 77; 78r; 101tr; 112l
Yalding Organic Gardens, Kent 93tr; 140 (photographer: Peter Anderson)

The publisher would also like to thank the following picture agencies and photographers for allowing their images to be reproduced for this book:

Adrian Fisher Mazes Ltd. 95r (Portman Lodge, Durweston, Dorset DT11 0QA, tel +44 (0) 1258 458845; fax +44 (0) 1258 488824; email: sales@mazemaker.com; www.fishermazes.com
Garden Exposures Photo Library 69b (RHS Chelsea Flower Show 2000); 92r (Chanel Garden)
Garden Picture Library 137b (Ron Sutherland/Westonbirt Festival)
Jenny Hendy 15 Japanese Garden (Walt Disney World, Florida); 18b (Giardino Corsini, Florence); 20t (Levens Hall, Cumbria); 21br (Wollerton Old Hall, Shropshire); 24b (Walt Disney World, Florida); 25b (EPCOT, Walt Disney World, Florida); 30 (Piet Bekaert's garden, Belgium); 32t (Houghton Lodge, Stockbridge, Hampshire); 32–33 (Walt Disney World, Florida); 33t (Levens Hall, Cumbria); 44b (Rofford Manor, Oxfordshire); 50b; 54tr (Château de Breteuil); 59tl (West Green

House, Hampshire/designer: Marylynn Abbott); 63t (Arley Hall, Cheshire); 63b; 71; 80t (designer W&F Van Glabbeek); 81bl (Chateau Fleury); 81br (Piet Bekaert's garden, Belgium); 83tr (Villa Gamberaia); 83br (Plas Brondanw, Gwynedd, Wales); 85bl (La Mormaire, France); 98l (La Mormaire, France); 101tl (La Mormaire, France)
John Glover 31b (RHS Hampton Court 2001 (designer: Nicholas Howard); 39 (Staatleg 31, Maarssen); 48t (Chatsworth, Derbyshire); 94–5 (Hever Castle, Kent); 96 (Petaluma, California, designed by Alex Champion); 96–97 (Parham, Surrey, designed by Adrian Fisher Mazes); 139 (The Dower House, Shropshire); 141t (The Manor House, Upton Grey, Hampshire)
Harpur Picture Library 66l (Manor House, Bledlow); 67 (Cambridge Botanic Garden);132r (William Barlow, RSA); 136b (design: Andrew Pfeiffer for Bill Taubman); 141b (Bourton House)
Mick Sharp 9b (Fishbourne Roman Palace, Chichester)
Photos Horticultural 31b (MJK)
Steve Wooster 11t (Piet Oudolf's garden); 85t (Les Jardins du Prieure Notre Dame d'Orsan); 92l (Woodpeckers);138 (Yalding Organic Gardens)

About the author: Jenny Hendy is a garden designer and plantswoman who has authored books on a wide range of topics. A childhood fascination for all things green and a zest for gardening eventually led her to study for an Honours degree in Botany. After having worked for one of Britain's leading gardening magazines, Jenny opted for a freelance career so that she could pursue her twin passions, writing and creating gardens. Soon after she became the first editor of the European Boxwood and Topiary Society's journal, Topiarius. In addition to designing landscapes, many with some element of topiary or green architecture, Jenny writes and lectures and is a guest contributor for BBC Radio.